HOW TO SAY no TO A STUBBORN HABIT

—even when you feel like saying Yes

Erwin W. Lutzer

While this book is designed for the reader's personal enjoyment and profit, it is also intended for group study. A Leader's Guide with Victor Multiuse Transparency Masters is available from your local Christian bookstore or from the publisher at $2.50.

VICTOR BOOKS

a division of SP Publications, Inc.
WHEATON. ILLINOIS 60187

Offices also in Fullerton, California • Whitby, Ontario, Canada • Amersham-on-the-Hill, Bucks, England

The author expresses appreciation to Moody Press and *Moody Monthly* magazine for their permission to quote from previous publications.

Scripture quotations are taken from the *New American Standard Version* (NASB) © 1960, 1962, 1963, 1968, 1971, 1972, 1973, the Lockman Foundation, La Habra, California. Used by permission.

Second printing, 1980

Recommended Dewey Decimal Classification: 241.3
Suggested subject headings: BEHAVIOR; CHRISTIAN LIFE; SIN; CONSCIENCE

Library of Congress Catalog Card Number: 79-64039
ISBN: 0-88207-787-2

VICTOR BOOKS
A division of SP Publications, Inc.
P.O. Box 1825 • Wheaton, Illinois 60187

*To Craig and Mora Bundy,
partners in sharing Christ's message
of hope and freedom*

CONTENTS

FOREWORD

I am happy to commend Erwin Lutzer's book, *How to Say No to a Stubborn Habit,* for the following reasons:

It is biblical. The author does not give easy answers to the problems arising from stubborn habits because he believes they have spiritual causes and therefore need spiritual answers found only in the Scriptures. Accordingly, he looks carefully into the biblical teaching relevant to the subject.

It is practical. Each chapter concludes with a suggested application. The reader is encouraged to take practical steps to apply what he has learned to his experience. This may take the form of a personal inventory, prayers for specific insight, or aids to developing study habits and relationships which will assist in achieving victory over the stubborn habit.

It is spiritual. There is no shortage of books in the self-improvement category and there are plenty of customers for such books. At first glance this book may appear to be yet another, but this is not the case. While some readers may want to break a habit to improve their figures or sweeten their breath, the author leads people to become what God created and redeemed them to be.

It is pastoral. Many case studies from the author's personal ministry are used to illustrate his principles. From these studies, the reader can discern a fine blend of compassion and firmness. The firmness has its roots in the authoritative Word of God and the compassion springs from the heart of one who struggles like all humans.

It is controversial. Readers will be stimulated to thought and discussion on a number of matters raised by the author. For example, the stubborn habits of the book title become sinful habits by the second paragraph of the preface. Are habits sinful or stubborn? The author's assertion that "self" and "the flesh" are the "same incurable desire to put our interests above God's" will undoubtedly lead some people to wonder about loving neighbor as we love self. The careful reader will also reconsider the balance between human responsibility and human susceptibility to such things as heredity and environment. All these topics need careful thought and the author's statement will help greatly.

D. Stuart Briscoe

Preface
A Hand from Heaven

Seneca cried, "Oh that a hand would come down from heaven and deliver me from my besetting sin!" His plea has been echoed throughout the centuries. We've all wished for the same miracle.

Sinful habits begin innocently enough, but if we don't master them, they will surely master us. We have all experienced the cycle: enjoy a forbidden pleasure, feel guilty, determine never to do it again, take pride in brief moments of self-control, then fail once more. Each time we repeat the pattern the ruts are cut a bit deeper, the chain pulls tighter.

Excusing our behavior because "we're just human," we become pessimistic, even defiant, and soon find ourselves victimized by a sin that refuses to budge. This behavior pattern becomes so familiar that eventually we don't even want to change. As we settle into an uneasy smugness, we come to feel at home in our anger, lust, worry, gluttony, laziness, bitterness, and selfishness—except for our small and occasional efforts at correction.

Can we really be delivered from the one-step-forward and two-backward routine? At times I've thought the answer was No. Despite my sincere attempts at yielding myself to God, I retained certain weaknesses (*sins* is a more honest word) that I concluded I would simply have to live with. After all, *no one* is perfect!

But I knew my private failure was no credit to Christ, who won the victory on the cross. Did He not promise that we could be *free indeed?* Through many failures and a few victories I've discovered that the most persistent sin can be dislodged. We can

9

be free from sins, even the ones safely tucked away in the crevices of our souls.

Imagine a city that is constantly being attacked at a vulnerable point along one of its walls. The enemy habitually exploits the same weakness—with startling success. Don't you think that the inhabitants would rebuild the defective fortification in preparation for the next assault? Yet countless Christians repeatedly succumb to the same temptations without a constructive program for strengthening their defenses. They have accepted failure as a way of life, reasoning, "That's just the way I am."

God has a different plan—for which He has given us a message of deliverance and hope. True, there are no easy miracles. Our success is neither instant nor automatic. Slick and easy solutions lead to false expectations which, in turn, spawn disappointment and unbelief. Applying biblical principles takes time and discipline. But steady progress is possible. Even long-established and sinful behavior patterns can be replaced by wholesome attitudes and actions.

Seneca did not know that his wish had been granted. God has come down from heaven to deliver us from our besetting sins. This book presents a step-by-step route to the freedom Christ has brought to us.

Let's explore it together.

Erwin W. Lutzer

1

WHY SO MUCH TEMPTATION?

"Why is lust so powerful?" Burt asked, crushed by the weight of his guilt. He had fallen into sexual sin. "How can I trust myself? . . . I don't want to live an immoral life. I promised myself I wouldn't do this but here I am again."

His question deserves an answer. Why is temptation so attractive, unrelenting, and powerful? Why doesn't God adjust the degree of our temptations so that the scales would be tipped more generously in our favor?

The Christian life does seem to be needlessly difficult at times. Surely God—the One who possesses all might and authority— could make it easier for those of us who love Him. Since so many believers succumb to one sin or another, often ending in ruin, it seems logical that God would keep a step ahead of us, diffusing the land mines along our path. If you are wondering how He could do this, consider these suggestions.

Satan Banned?

First, God could eliminate the devil. In fact, if He had done that at the time of Creation, chances are that Adam and Eve would not have plunged the human race into sin. Most likely our first parents would have obeyed God without pausing to consider the fruit of the forbidden tree.

Assuming Adam and Eve were free agents, why didn't God give them the opportunity to choose without outside interference? The serpent was beautiful, seemed to speak with authority, and promised a better life. As far as we know, Adam and Eve had not been told about the existence of Satan, and so were quite unprepared for this abrupt encounter. If the serpent had been barred from the Garden, Adam and Eve would have been more inclined to obey God. They might have chosen not to eat from the forbidden tree.

The presence of Satan in the Garden and his activity on our planet tips the scales in favor of evil choices. I'm not saying we must follow his sinister suggestions; but if he were banned from the earth, we could resist temptation much more easily.

Much of the evil in the world, including our own struggles, can be traced to the interference of unseen spiritual forces. If God were to annihilate the devil, or at least confine him to the pit, we could take giant steps in our walk with the King. No more of the one-step-forward, two-backward routine! Our battle with temptation would be minimized and we'd be more inclined to resist the enticement of sin. Why doesn't God obliterate Satan?

Dampened Passions?

A second suggestion to minimize the casualty toll in the Christian life would be for God to dull the arrows of temptation that harass us from inside. James wrote, "But each one is tempted when he is carried away and enticed by his own lust" (James 1:14). Could not God dampen those passions to make moral purity more easily within reach?

You and I were born with a sinful nature which combines response to outward stimuli with its inner twisted passions of greed, selfishness, anger, rebellion, and lust. Every honest

Christian admits to being overcome by one or more of these desires at some point in his or her spiritual pilgrimage. Surely God, who knows our frailty, could dampen those passions just a bit. Then we'd be more likely to be victorious, and a credit to our Redeemer.

We've all heard someone say, "I know what I ought to do, but just can't. I've tried, asked God to help me, and have still failed." Paul wrote about his own struggle, "For that which I am doing, I do not understand; for I am not practicing what I would like to do, but I am doing the very thing I hate" (Rom. 7:15). The church reformer, John Knox, wrote these words before he died: "Now, after many battles, I find nothing in me but vanity and corruption. For in quietness I am negligent, in trouble impatient, tending to desperation; pride and ambition assault me on the one part, covetousness and malice trouble me on the other; briefly, O Lord, the affections of the flesh do almost suppress the operation of Thy Spirit." If this man of God had such struggles, is there hope for the rest of us?

Rearranged Schedules?

Even if God did not banish the devil or dull our sinful passions, couldn't He guide us away from the places of temptation? Then we could be protected from circumstances that would provoke us to sin.

Didn't David sin with Bathsheba because she happened to be taking a bath next door while the king was resting on the rooftop? It seems that God could have arranged for her to take her bath two hours earlier, or an hour later. Surely a sovereign God would have no difficulty in rearranging the schedules of His finite creatures.

Didn't Achan sin because he saw a Babylonian garment left unattended after the siege of Jericho? Didn't Abraham lie because there was a famine in the land and he feared for his life? Didn't

Samson divulge his secret because of his attraction to the charming Delilah?

God does not shield us from circumstances that provoke us to sin. Remember it was the Holy Spirit who led Christ into the wilderness to be tempted of the devil. In the Lord's Prayer Jesus taught the disciples to pray, "And do not lead us into temptation, but deliver us from evil" (Matt. 16:13). We are to ask God to preserve us from situations where we might be vulnerable to sin. Yet we must admit, God does lead us into circumstances that potentially could provoke us to sin.

Of course, I'm not saying that God causes us to sin; nor does He tempt us as Satan does. James wrote, "Let no one say when he is tempted, 'I am being tempted by God' for God cannot be tempted by evil, and He Himself does not tempt anyone" (James 1:13). We can never blame God for what we do. If we sin, it is because of our sinful nature; therefore we are responsible. But God does *test* us; He also allows Satan to tempt us. Quite unintentionally on our part, we find ourselves in situations that are an outward stimulus to sin.

A woman trying desperately to break the habit of smoking said that she was making progress until she was transferred to an office where everyone smoked. In an atmosphere drenched with the smell of tobacco, she fell back into her former habit.

After meeting a former boyfriend, a married woman discovered that she was falling deeply in love with him. Consequently, she began to think she had married the wrong man, and felt trapped. Now she asks, "Why did God, who knows how weak I am, allow us to meet again?"

A homosexual admitted that he had begun his sexual relationships with other men when, at the age of 12, he was seduced by an older homosexual. So began a long struggle with abnormal behavior. Could not God have protected him from his experience?

Alcoholics, trying to stay dry, often slip back into drunkenness because of pressure from peers who are addicted to the bottle. So it goes.

And what about the more subtle sins of the mind? Yes, Christ taught that evil originates in the heart, but many of our struggles with evil thoughts are provoked by our environment. All around us are stimuli which draw out the worst in us. Without taking us out of the world, God could lead us to circumstances less conducive to evil passions, covetousness, and anger. If at least some of the chuckholes were removed from our paths, the possibility of blowouts would be lessened.

good thought

But God has not shielded us from the places or the power of cruel temptations. Satan has access to our lives; our sin nature is unrestricted, and often without warning we find ourselves in situations that contribute to outward or secret sin.

So we are back to Burt's question—why is temptation so powerful?

Some Reasons for Temptation

A Test of Loyalty

As might be expected, God has a purpose in allowing us to be tempted. To begin, *let's remember that temptation, with all of its frightful possibilities for failure, is God's method of testing our loyalties.* We cannot say that we love someone until we have had to make some hard choices on his behalf. Similarly, we cannot say we love God unless we've said No to persistent temptations.

Take Abraham as an example. God asked him to slay his favorite son. He was strongly tempted to say No to God. The altar he built was probably the most carefully constructed one ever made. As he worked, he surely thought of numerous reasons why he should disobey God: Isaac was needed to fulfill God's promise, Sarah would never understand, and above all, how could a merciful God expect a man to slay his own beloved son?

Of course, you know how the story ended. Abraham passed the test; the angel of the Lord prevented him from stabbing his son. Notice God's evaluation of the incident: "Now I know that you fear God, since you have not withheld your son, your only son, from Me" (Gen. 22:12).

How do we know Abraham loved God? *Because he chose to say Yes when all the powers of hell and the passions of his soul were crying No.* This fierce temptation gave Abraham a striking opportunity to prove his love for the Almighty.

Let's return to some of those situations we mentioned earlier. What about the woman who seemingly cannot resist falling in love with another man? Or the alcoholic tempted by his friends to revert back to his old habits? Or the young man surrounded by the wrong crowd? Why does God not shield us from these circumstances? He is allowing us the luxury of difficult choices so that we can prove our love for Him. These are our opportunities to choose God rather than the world.

Do you love God? I'm glad you said Yes. But what happens when you are confronted with a tough decision—such as whether you should satisfy your passions or control them? Our response to temptation is an accurate barometer of our love for God. One of the first steps in handling temptation is to see it as an opportunity to test our loyalties. If we love the world, the love of the Father is not in us (1 John 2:15). Each temptation leaves us better or worse; neutrality is impossible.

That's why God doesn't exterminate the devil. Admittedly, the presence of wicked spirits in the world does make our choices more difficult. But think of what such agonizing choices mean to God. We prove our love for God when we say Yes to Him, even when the deck appears to be stacked against us.

What it boils down to is this: do we value the pleasures of the world or those that come from God? The opportunities for sin that pop up around us, the sinful nature within us, and the demonic forces around us give us numerous opportunities to answer that question.

Transformed Passions

A second reason God does not make our choices easier is because *temptation is His character development curriculum.* Sinful habits are a millstone about our necks, a blotch on our lives. But that's only half the story! Our temptations, struggles, and yes, even our sins are used by God to help us climb the ladder of spiritual maturity. If you see your sinful struggles only as a liability, you will never learn all that God wants to teach you through them.

There is a saying of Goethe, the German poet, that talent is formed in solitude, but character in the storms of life. God wants to do something more beautiful in your life than simply give you victory over a sin. He wants to replace that sin with the positive qualities of a fruitful life.

Temptation is God's magnifying glass; it shows us how much work He has left to do in our lives. When the Israelites were wandering in the wilderness, God let them become hungry and thirsty; on one occasion they were without water for three days. They became disappointed with their slow pace of travel; they were impatient with Moses' long rendezvous on the mountain. Why didn't God meet their expectations? Listen to Moses' commentary. God did all this "that He might humble you, testing you, to know what was in your heart, whether you would keep His commandments or not" (Deut. 8:2b).

There it is again—God allowed the Israelites to suffer temptation to test their loyalties and to bring out their latent sinfulness. Temptation brings out the best or the worst in us. The Israelites didn't realize how rebellious they were until they got hungry. Temptation brings the impurities to the surface. Then God begins the siphoning process.

Sometimes God teaches us these lessons by letting us suffer the consequences of our own sin. James wrote that we are enticed by our own lust. That word *entice* carries with it the imagery of a hunter who puts out bait for wild animals. The mouse can see no valid reason why he should not eat that piece of cheese. Since his knowledge is limited, he cannot predict the future and he doesn't understand traps. So he eats, and suffers a fatal outcome. Some of us, thinking we can predict the consequences of our actions, assign a more serious result to overt sins than to those confined to thought and imagination. But even the sins of the mind exact their toll, and ultimately we no longer control the sin; it controls us. In time God may dry up our fountains of pleasure and ambition so that we will turn to Him in repentance.

When we do, God leads us to something better. He wants to develop within us the rich character qualities called the fruit of the Spirit: love, joy, and peace, to name a few. God's purpose is to conform us to the image of His Son. To accomplish this, our character deficiencies (*sins* is a better word) must be brought to the surface so that we can be changed.

Temptation means risk. The potential for devastating failure is ever with us. But precisely because the stakes are so high, the rewards of resisting are great. We cannot say No to temptation without saying Yes to something far better.

Strength for Our Weakness

Finally, *God uses our sins to show us His grace and power*. The depressing effect of sin is offset by the good news of God's grace. Paul wrote, "And the Law came in that the transgression might increase; but where sin increased, grace abounded all the more" (Rom. 5:20).

Paul was given a thorn in the flesh so that he would remain humble. Perhaps it was a temptation he struggled to resist. He asked God three times for deliverance, but God said, "My grace is sufficient for you, for power is perfected in weakness" (2 Cor. 12:9a). Paul, therefore, boasted about his weakness, knowing that it provided an opportunity for God's power to rest upon him. "For when I am weak, then am I strong" (v. 10b). If you are beset by an especially obstinate sin, you may be on the verge of seeing God's grace displayed in your life. Although you may now be preoccupied with your struggle, you may soon be preoccupied with your God.

God strikes at the core of our motivations. He is not interested in merely applying a new coat of paint, imposing a new set of rules. He wants to rebuild our minds and give us new values. The most important part of us is that which nobody sees, except God. And He wants to begin His work there.

Think about that one particular sin of yours—the one that won't move off center stage. Maybe it's an obvious one: drunkenness, gluttony, or sexual misconduct. Or maybe it's a very private sin, the one in your mind: pride, anxiety, fear, or bitterness. Perhaps your imagination would make an X rated movie look censored. Or you may have a personality quirk, a feeling of deep-seated inferiority, or an uncontrollable temper.

Whatever it is, God can deliver you from that sin. You and He can track it down, route and exterminate it. Sin need not have dominion over you. You can be sure that God will never take from you something that is good. Rather, when you are ready, He will remove the evil and replace it with something far better. He will tear down your fortress so that He can build a palace in its place.

Are you ready for such a transformation? The next chapter will help you to answer that question.

Suggested Application

1. Take inventory of your life by asking: What is my most persistent temptation? Why is it so difficult to say No to this temptation and Yes to God?

2. Read the story of Christ's temptation in the desert (Matt. 4:1–11). List all of the reasons why Christ might have found it easy to give in to Satan's suggestions. Speculate as to what the consequences of such an act would have been. Contrast this with how the Israelites acted when they were hungry (Ex. 16; Num. 11). What can we learn from the contrast between Israel and Christ?

3. Before you read the next chapter, spend some quiet time in prayer with your special temptation or sin in mind. Ask God for wisdom in the following three areas.

　a. that you will be able to properly identify the *cause* of your defeat

　b. that God will give you wisdom in planning a specific course of action to overcome the problem

　c. that you will have the persistence to follow that action to its completion.

4. Take a few moments of each day to thank God for what He is going to do in your life and, particularly, how He is going to show His strength and grace at the point of your weakness.

2

THE GROUND RULES

Can God change people? Yes, He can, but He always does it on His terms. Before you can take steps toward positive change, there are three basic conditions you *must* accept. If you falter in accepting any one of them, you will not progress toward freedom from your sinful habit. What are these essentials?

The First Condition

First, *you must believe that God is good.* Because of the evils that exist in the world, the goodness of God is one of the most difficult doctrines to accept. Yet unless we wholeheartedly believe in it, we are paralyzed in our Christian growth.

It is not surprising that Satan's first move in the Garden of Eden was to cause Eve to doubt the goodness of God. Here are his words: "You surely shall not die! For God knows that in the day you eat from it your eyes will be opened, and you will be like God, knowing good and evil" (Gen. 3:4–5). His point was: "God is restricting you because He doesn't want you to achieve your potential! You have the inherent right to be like Him, but He won't let you—He isn't on your side at all."

Satan convinced Eve to believe that God did not have her best interests at heart—that He would hold her back from developing her potential. Eve believed the lie.

Today, Satan uses similar strategy to make us dissatisfied with God's will for us. Our anger at circumstances and our rebellion against God's commandments stem from our lack of confidence in God's goodness. The single girl asks: "How can God be good? If He were, He'd give me companionship. Doesn't He know how lonely I am?"

The playboy reasons, "Why should God restrict me from pleasure? When I'm hungry I eat; when I want pleasure I have sex. A God who cramps my lifestyle isn't good. And if He were, He'd see that I find somebody to really satisfy me."

The alcoholic complains, "If God were good He'd give me a decent job. After all, wasn't it financial pressure that drove me to drink? Why doesn't God get me out of this mess? God is good? Good for what?"

I counseled a woman who needed to confess the sin of bitterness. Her response, "If God loves me, why did He allow my parents to treat me like they did? A good God would never have allowed this to happen!" Did she get rid of her bitterness? No. She couldn't forgive her parents because she couldn't "forgive" God.

If you are a worrier, you doubt God's goodness. You are afraid God will bring circumstances into your life that are not in your best interests. If you are greedy and covetous, you doubt whether God is being fair with you. If you experience uncontrollable anger, you are rebelling against God's will for your life.

Look at that sin that you don't want to give up; growing in the roots of your stubbornness is your doubt about God's goodness. You do not trust Him to do the best for you, because *your way* is better.

Let's return to the story in the Garden of Eden for a moment. Notice how Satan focused on a restriction and used it to blind Eve to God's blessing. Yes, there was one tree she could not enjoy, but presumably there were hundreds she could. Did Satan point out the many trees she was permitted to eat from? Hardly. He focused on one negative and Eve forgot God's generosity and grace. So it is today. Satan will urge you to focus on one issue, one aggravation, one restriction. At that moment, he'll try to convince you that God's way is not best, but takes second place to what he can offer you.

Do you doubt God's goodness? Are you fully prepared to accept that the will of God is perfect and acceptable? What would you think if God did take away that one desire, that one weakness? If He did deliver you from sensual thoughts, would you feel cheated? If He denied you the pleasure of marriage, would you feel ripped off? If you became victorious over cigarettes or alcohol, would you be resentful because you had been denied a bit of pleasure?

Perhaps now you are beginning to understand why you cannot begin to break your sinful habit unless you believe in God's goodness. The reason is simple: if you doubt God's goodness you will not want to change. You'll be convinced that God wants to rob you rather than enrich you.

I've discovered that the most frustrating problem in helping those who come for counsel is simply that most people do not really want to change. Of course, they are prepared to make minor adjustments—particularly if their behavior is getting them into trouble. But most of them are comfortable with their sin as long as it doesn't get out of hand. And often they'd prefer to have God keep His activity in their lives to a minimum.

What causes this lack of enthusiasm for getting rid of sin? We are afraid that some worthwhile pleasure will pass us by. We question whether God's way is indeed the best.

If you doubt God's goodness, you will not only resist change but will also fear it. A young man I counseled simply could not give his future to God for fear that God might require him to drop out of medical school. He doubted whether God's will for him would be the best.

Countless Christians resist surrender to God, frightened at what God might ask them to do. He might lead them to the mission field, let them remain single, or require that they give up their love of money or their pursuit of sinful pleasures.

When you doubt God's goodness, you hug sins tightly to your bosom, afraid that God will rob you of your crutch, your pastime, your pleasure. Occasionally, you are stirred to give up your sin, but soon find you can't risk the loss.

But is your way really better than God's? Was Satan the good guy in the Garden of Eden? And God the villain? Jesus put the matter straight, "The thief comes only to steal, and kill, and destroy; I came that they might have life, and might have it abundantly" (John 10:10). To believe your way is better than God's is to take your place with Eve and believe Satan's lie. No matter how many pleasures Satan offers you, his ultimate intention is to ruin you. *Your* destruction is his highest priority.

On the positive side, if you accept the fact that God is good, two results will follow: (1) you can surrender to Him without reservations or fear of being gypped, and (2) you will thirst for change, knowing that the watering holes of the world cannot compare with the refreshing water that Christ promises. Are you prepared to accept what you know, deep down in yourself, that God's plan is perfect? If so, you will be prepared to part with your sin, knowing that God will replace it with something better. You'll have passed the first test as a candidate for radical change.

The Second Condition

What is the second essential truth you must accept? It is that *you are fully responsible for your behavior*. All of us are born with a propensity to avoid blame. Children display a remarkable ability to shift responsibility to others. My wife and I have observed that our children can spontaneously, creatively, almost ingeniously, invent excuses for their misbehavior.

It began in Eden. God asked Adam, "Have you eaten from the tree of which I commanded you not to eat?" The question was straightforward, and could have been answered in one word, "Yes." But Adam responded, "The woman whom Thou gavest to be with me, she gave me from the tree, and I ate" (Gen. 3:11–12).

Read those words again. What Adam really said was, "It's Your fault—I'm stuck with this weak-willed woman You created." So Adam blamed both God and his wife before he admitted that he also was party to the deed.

Notice his logic. God created the woman, the woman ate the fruit, and then gave it to him. He believed that if God had not created Eve, or if Eve would not have disobeyed, he would not have sinned. Hence he was not blameworthy. In accepting responsibility, Eve fared no better. She said, "The serpent deceived me, and I ate" (v. 13b). She wasn't responsible either. Someone has well said, "Adam blamed Eve; Eve blamed the serpent; and the serpent didn't have a leg to stand on!" No one was responsible; it was God's fault.

Was it? True, God created the tree, the woman, the man, and even Lucifer, who became the devil. God could have created a garden without this forbidden tree and could have barred Satan from entry. Yes, a sovereign God could have done it all differently. But *Eve made a choice and so did Adam*. Thus they must bear the full responsibility for their choice. The serpent also gets his due—each made a choice, each deserves blame. In the Garden, the matter of human responsibility was settled forever: each individual must take responsibility for his choices.

Of course, we must be sensitive when speaking about these matters. Some people are disturbed because they have suffered physical and emotional abuse. Others follow a life of sin because of the warped values of their parents. To some extent, we are all products of our heredity and environment. But even allowing for this, we know that civilized society cannot long exist unless there is an assumption of individual responsibility for one's actions. We are all accountable, to family, employer, society, church, and ultimately to God. Every mature person needs to stop blaming and begin taking full responsibility for what he is—past, present, and future.

A prominent American said of the assassin of Robert Kennedy, "I do not blame him, but the society that produced him." Will Rogers once aptly remarked that there are two eras in American history—the passing of the buffalo and the passing of the buck!

We cannot exaggerate the harm that has come to individuals from the teaching of Sigmund Freud that those who misbehave are sick. We do not hold people responsible for catching the flu, measles, or having cancer. We have hospitals, not prisons, for the physically sick, simply because they bear no moral blame for their illness. The reprehensible Freudian implication is clear: if we are not responsible for physical illness, why should we be blamed for crime, a symptom of mental illness?

To say that a rapist, murderer, or thief is sick, is to conclude that he should not be subject to punishment. After all, he simply caught a strange disease—he is the victim of forces beyond his control.

Recently, my wife and I watched a TV interview with a doctor who argued that the peculiarities of our behavior stem from our birth experience. If a baby is born in a noisy, bright, and seemingly unfriendly delivery room, he will develop hostility in his adult life. It follows that no one should be blamed for hostility.

If a teenager is in trouble, it's the parents' fault—they were too strict or too lenient. Or perhaps it was his environment—he was brought up in a wealthy home. Everyone knows that wealth spawns boredom and boredom breeds crime. Conversely, he is not responsible because he came from a poor home—poverty drives a man to drugs, sex, and crime. Even in a prison, it is hard to find a person who considers himself guilty.

The schools of modern psychiatry based on this unbiblical principle have fared poorly in helping with emotional problems. Such psychiatrists have become professional excuse-finders, sifting through the rubble of the past, the pressures of the present, and the anxieties of the future, searching for a doorstep where the blame can be placed.

How contrary to the Scriptures! The Bible calls each individual a sinner. We are fully responsible for our choices. Although that's a tough pill to swallow, it is basic to our hope that God can change us. After all, if we are responsible, we are in control of our choices. We can change. And we can choose to let God change us!

Let's take the serious problem of homosexuality as an example. A man told me that his abnormal desires began at puberty, but not through association with a practicing homosexual. Rather, there were unhealthy factors in his home that were so conducive to perverted thinking and behavior that this young man grew up believing that he had been born a homosexual. In his words—"predestined to be weird."

Can he change to heterosexual feeling and behavior? Not if he blames his environment or his genes for his actions. This man did change. Listen to his words: "For years I believed that I could never change because I was a homosexual by constitution, not by choice. I took no responsibility for my behavior. But as I began to read the Scriptures, I began to believe God could change me. The first step in that direction was when I took full responsibility for my homosexual behavior. No excuses; no alibis."

Alcoholics are known for their ability to avoid responsibility for their behavior. The wife, a boss, their friends, or their neighborhood is to blame.

However the Bible teaches that each person is responsible. No one can make you promiscuous, or give you an ulcer. These behavioral patterns are not caused by circumstances, but rather by *your response to circumstances*. And even in those instances where you are propelled by passions seemingly beyond your control, you still do the choosing. Hence, you are accountable.

The doorway to hope begins to open as you take responsibility for your sins, admitting your guilt. When you call something sin, there is the possibility of deliverance—for Christ came to call sinners to repentance. As Jay Adams wrote, "To call homosexuality a sickness, for example, does not raise the client's hope. But to call homosexuality a sin, as the Bible does, is to offer hope" (Jay E. Adams, *Competent to Counsel,* Grand Rapids: Baker Book House, 1970, p. 139).

When you assume responsibility for your sin you find that you are now a candidate for God's mercy and power. A friend of mine put it this way: "God occasionally cures illness, but He has a sure cure for sin." Assuming responsibility also restores your God-given dignity. God did not create you as a victim of your circumstances, nor even as the slave of your genetic makeup. You can rise above your past and need not be pushed into any mold—whether it be one of environment or heredity.

Like Adam, we are all tempted to say, "The parents whom Thou gavest me . . ." Or, "The friends Thou gavest me . . ." Or, "The passions Thou gavest me . . ." Many people have spent a small fortune for professional counseling to explore problems that they could have solved if they had been willing—and helped—to accept responsibility for their actions.

If you are still squirming, maybe trying to explain why your situation is unique, complaining that I don't understand how badly you were mistreated or why you were caught in a particular habit, then you have probably failed the second test for admittance to God's character-changing program. Only the person who says, "*I* have sinned," reaches to receive His mercy and grace.

The Third Condition

If you've made it thus far, you have at least one more proposition to accept to begin working on that stubborn habit. Quite simply, it is this: *you must believe that deliverance is possible.* To Adam and Eve, who sinned so flagrantly, God made a promise that Satan's power would be crushed. "And I will put enmity between you and the woman, and between your seed and her seed; He shall bruise you on the head, and you shall bruise Him on the heel" (Gen. 3:15). The message was clear: in the conflict, Satan would only nip Christ's heel, whereas Christ would bruise the serpent's head. Victory over sin and Satan is a possibility for the Christian.

The New Testament is above all else a Book of hope. It details how God fulfilled this promise. There is no sin—no, not one—that must of necessity crush you. God has dramatically provided a way of escape.

"No temptation has overtaken you but such as is common to man; and God is faithful, who will not allow you to be tempted beyond what you are able, but with the temptation will provide the way of escape also, that you may be able to endure it" (1 Cor. 10:13). In this verse we notice two facts.

• You cannot plead that your case is unique or special. True, no two situations are identical, but your basic struggles against the passions of the world, your sinful nature, and Satan are the same as those others have faced. You can take comfort in the fact that you are experiencing a temptation that someone else has already faced—successfully. Joseph did not succumb to lust; Moses conquered pride; Elijah overcame depression.

But what of people involved in the more stubborn sins of idolatry, adultery, homosexuality, drunkenness, or kleptomania? The New Testament church at Corinth had these kinds of people—who had been freed from their sin. Paul listed the above sins and then added, "And such were some of you; but you were washed, but you were sanctified, but you were justified in the name of the Lord Jesus Christ, and in the Spirit of our God" (1 Cor. 6:11). Your situation is not unique. Someone has already faced your problem victoriously.

• Paul asserted that God will give you the resources to cope with all temptations. A faithful God does not expect you to do what you cannot; He supplies the needed strength. If you say, "I know what I have to do, but can't," what then?

Do you remember the story of the battle between the Children of Israel and Amalek? When it was time for the battle, Moses said, "I will station myself on the top of the hill with the staff of God in my hand . . . So it came about when Moses held his hand up, that Israel prevailed, and when he let his hand down, Amalek prevailed. But Moses' hands were heavy. Then they took a stone and put it under him, and he sat on it and Aaron and Hur supported his hands, one on one side and one on the other. Thus his hands were steady until the sun set." After this battle, "Moses built an altar, and named it, The Lord is My Banner" (Ex. 17:9–15).

If you truly believe that you can't do what you should, then you need help from the people of God. You need someone to hold up your weak arms, to help you walk a straight path, to comfort, to give strength, to pray for you. However, if you say, "I can't" and let it go at that, you are calling into question the integrity of God's character or the validity of your own faith.

Why is it so essential for you to believe that victory over your sin is possible? Simply because *no one can win a war he believes can't be won!* To go to battle believing in advance that there can be no permanent victory, is to succumb to the enemy before the campaign gets under way.

We Christians have often conceded to the enemy by assuming that some sins cannot be dislodged. Such unbelief breeds pessimism, disobedience, and despair. The teaching of the New Testament is that all things are possible with God to him who believes.

Name your sin right now and say, "Thank You, God, that deliverance from it is possible!" God has had a vast amount of experience in delivering His people from temptation. Peter wrote, "The Lord knows how to rescue the godly from temptation, and to keep the unrighteous under punishment for the day of judgment" (2 Peter 2:9).

Are you prepared to believe that God is good? that you are a responsible person? and that you can win victory over that stubborn sin?

Suggested Application

This chapter identifies three necessary conditions you must accept if you want to say No to temptation and mean it. Here are some assignments to help you accept these basic truths.

1. God is good. Affirm your belief in God's goodness by reading the following verses: Exodus 33:19 and 34:6; Psalms 27:13; 31:19; 34:8; 65:4; 86:5; 106:1; 107:8–9; 145:7; James 1:17. (Choose any two of these verses and memorize them.)

2. You are fully responsible for your behavior. No doubt David spent time finding excuses for his sin with Bathsheba. For example, unexpected circumstances led him to notice her just when her husband was out of town. God could have controlled those circumstances. Read David's prayer of repentance in Psalm 51 with these questions in mind:

- What evidence is there that David finally took full responsibility for what he had done?
- What evidence is there that David realized that sin is more serious than simply whether one hurts someone else?

Now read Romans 1:18–32. Trace the spiral of sin by asking, *Why* is man responsible for his behavior?

3. Deliverance is possible. What sin do you think is the most difficult to overcome? Now read Luke 1:37; John 8:32; and Hebrews 3:12. Why do you think that we so often fail in tapping God's resources?

4. Try to think of biblical illustrations of those who successfully resisted temptation. Why were they successful?

3

PUTTING YOUR PAST BEHIND YOU

For of all sad words of tongue or pen, The saddest are these: "It might have been." John Greenleaf Whittier

"It might have been" has a way of catching up with you. We've all known how painful regret can be—especially when lives are deeply affected. A teenager blows his mind on drugs; an alcoholic leaves his wife and children; a Christian's life is wasted in the pursuit of greedy ambition. These situations, and dozens like them, trigger painful regret.

Regardless of how sheltered or permissive our past, all of us have had regrets accompanied with feelings of guilt. "If only I had not met that man . . . If only I had chosen different friends . . . If only . . ."

You must deal with your past before you can experience freedom in the future. The sin that troubles you today sank its roots into your life yesterday. You can't break your sinful habits until you have a new beginning.

Satan is particularly adept at using your past to ruin your future. His weapon is the illegitimate use of guilt feelings. Sins multiply in the soil of discouragement. One offense easily leads to another. You are caught in a vicious circle until you realize that your past need not control your future. God promises a new beginning.

When I attended grade school in Canada, we often played "Fox and Goose" on the fresh, clean snow in the schoolyard. After about 15 minutes the trails became so messy that we'd move to a clean area and stake out new paths in the glistening snow. Soon we'd have to move again, and then again, always searching for a fresh beginning.

I observed something at that time that has stayed with me. Whenever we blazed a new trail, all of us children were anxious to stay within its bounds, but after the trail became wide and untidy, we were less careful about spoiling the pattern in the snow. In fact, after about 10 minutes of rowdy play we didn't care how the trails looked. We even deliberately made the playing area as messy as possible.

What a picture of mankind! I think of a young Christian woman who expressed sincere desire to serve God. Her way of life was prudent, respectable, and moral. But then contrary to her intentions, she succumbed to sexual sin. She felt overwhelmed with guilt and the realization that she could never recover her virginity. Thinking that a new beginning was impossible, she threw all caution to the winds and sought sexual excitement with different partners. When this girl became pregnant, she did not even know who had fathered the child.

So it is with many who become trapped in one sin or another. Sinful habits have a domino effect—if you do it once, you might as well go all the way as often as you like. That's why some Christians question whether God can change them. They believe they cannot live differently in the future because of the past.

Satan delights in this kind of logic. He wants you to think that you have gone too far, that since the past cannot be reclaimed, you might as well give up. James Stalker, the Scottish preacher, wrote, "The great tempter of men has two lies with which he plies us at two different stages. Before we have fallen, he tells us that one fall does not matter; it is a trifle; we can easily recover ourselves again. After we have fallen, he tells us that it is hopeless; we are given over to sin, and need not attempt to rise.''

Stalker goes on to explain that both of these notions are false. *One sin does matter*. Even one fall can cause you to lose something that can never be recovered. An equisite vessel can be broken and mended, but it will never be the same. Also, one sin leads to others. It's like climbing up an icy hill. Even as you attempt to rise, you fall again.

But when you do fall, you dare not accept Satan's second lie, namely, that there is no use in attempting to rise. Your enemy wants you to believe that since the past cannot be reclaimed, there is no way to break with its power.

Can you have a new beginning? In one sense, No, since the past cannot be relived. Virginity cannot be recovered; ruined health from nicotine, drugs, or gluttony will have to be accepted. Some broken homes may never be pieced back together. But in a deeply profound sense, you can have a new beginning. God offers two precious commodities: (1) genuine forgiveness, a blotting out of all your sins—past, present, and future; and (2) the assurance that your past need not control your future. The cycle of sin can be broken. You can rise again.

Listen to God's promise to a nation possessed with violence, deceit, and sensual corruption. '' 'Come now, and let us reason together,' says the Lord. 'Though your sins are as scarlet, they will be as white as snow; though they are red like crimson, they will be like wool' '' (Isa. 1:18).

Although a messy "Fox and Goose" trail can not be straightened out, a fresh blanket of snow can cover it. *You too can have a new beginning*. The spoiled paths, the soiled places in your life can be covered by forgiveness. "Your sins . . . will be white as snow.''

The Consequences of Guilt

To deal with the past is to deal with guilt. Guilt feelings can be like a millstone around your neck, keeping you tied to your sins and wedded to past failures. Sometimes your conscience may trouble you, rehearsing the sins of your past in vivid detail. Or you may just have a vague feeling of guilt, a confirmed suspicion that you've blown it again and will always be a second-class citizen in the kingdom of heaven.

Living with guilt is like trying to drive your car with the brakes on. Guilt feelings can produce many serious consequences.

• Physical illness is often caused by suppressed guilt. Some doctors have estimated that nearly one-half of their patients could be released if they could be told with authority, "You are forgiven." Christian Psychologist Gary Collins has written, "The mere energy of keeping the guilt out of one's mind can put a strain on the body and cause it to break down."

• Unresolved guilt causes depression. Feelings of hopelessness and worthlessness are generated by the nagging feeling that "you've blown it," and since the past cannot be reclaimed, there is little use trying to live a fruitful life.

• Guilt is often the cause for lack of faith in God. First John 3:21 reads, "Beloved if our heart does not condemn us, we have confidence toward God." I've discovered in my counseling ministry that perhaps the most widespread cause of doubt is guilt. A person who feels impure will struggle with trust in God.

• Guilt causes people to punish themselves. For example, some parents whose children have gone astray do not want to be free from guilt. They believe *they* must pay for their children's behavior, and that guilt is the price of the ticket. Others take this a step further and interpret every tragedy as God's way of punishing them; some actually long to become physically sick so that they will have the satisfaction of paying for their sins. Such guilt feelings are never appeased.

• Guilt often causes people to do good works. A husband brings his wife flowers in the evening because he has shouted angrily at her in the morning. Others give money to the church or are extra kind to a needy friend, hoping to atone for their sins. Some children who have rebelled against their parents become burdened for social concerns and even work in the ghetto. Rather than ask their parents' forgiveness, they unconsciously assume that their sacrificial spirit will balance the books.

But good works never erase guilt. Good activity can suppress guilt, can help you to deny it, or to buy time with your conscience, but the guilt will soon surface in another form. A friend of mine says that it's like spilling ketchup on your tie. Resolutions to be more careful next time, or even the determination to become a self-sacrificing slave, will never erase the stain. Until a remedy is found that can be applied to the guilt directly, it is there to stay. Fortunately, God has not left you without hope.

Principles for Handling Guilt

God's will for you is that you be free from all forms of guilt. He who is rich in mercy anticipated your moral and emotional entanglements. Fortunately, God is never taken by surprise. He offers you freedom from a nagging conscience. Let me suggest three steps toward finding this freedom.

1. Identify the cause of your guilt feelings. Often this can be done easily—an immoral relationship, cheating on your income tax, a harsh word to your parents—all these sources of guilt are quite easy to identify. Perhaps you will want to list these causes on a sheet of paper and then deal with each one specifically to put it behind you, once and for all.

Let me warn you that sometimes people experience false guilt, bringing torment upon themselves for matters beyond their control. A woman and her three-year-old daughter stood at a curb, waiting to cross the street. The child asked, "Mother, can I

go now?'' Absentmindedly the mother answered, "Yes."
Seconds later, she watched in horror as her three-year-old
daughter was crushed to death by an oncoming truck. The horror
of that event will never be erased from this woman's mind.

She is plagued with guilt, an incredible feeling of regret and
anger at herself. These feelings came because the woman could
not forgive herself. God does not convict you for an error in
judgment, but rather for consciously choosing to sin. This
woman needs to forgive herself and to realize that self-
incrimination is not what God desires.

To deal with guilt feelings, bring them into the open where you
can deal with them. Then ask yourself honestly, *Why do I feel
guilty?*

2. *Realize that God's remedy for sin is complete.* In Christ,
God anticipated all of your feelings, discouragements, and
failures. Christ's death on the cross included a sacrifice for all our
sins—past, present, and future. Every sin you will ever commit
has already been paid for. All of your sins were future when
Christ died 2,000 years ago. There is no sin that you will ever
commit which has not *already* been included in Christ's death
(see Col. 2:13).

God does not find it hard to forgive. It is not as though He
regrets giving you a second chance. The price for forgiveness has
already been paid, and God wants you to accept it freely.

An atheist asked Billy Graham, "If Hitler had received Christ
on his deathbed, would he have gone to heaven, whereas
someone who lived a good life but rejected Christ would go to
hell?'' That is a trick question. It was asked in such a way as to
make the Gospel appear ridiculous. But the answer is Yes. If
Hitler accepted Christ, God could forgive him completely,
because Christ's death included all of Hitler's sins! God values
Christ so much that He could accept Hitler with Christ's merit,
but He cannot accept the best person without Christ's merit!

Visualize the worst sin imaginable—Christ died for *that* sin.

The cry from the Cross—"It is finished"—is but one word in Greek—*tetelestai,* a word used in business transactions. When this word was written across a bill, it meant "Paid in full." You need never try to make up for your sins on your own. Christ's death paid for your sins *in full*.

When God forgives you, your sins are blotted out so completely that He does not remember them; He never holds them against you again. The sins you confessed yesterday will never again be a barrier between you and God—unless you refuse to accept God's forgiveness or doubt the value of Christ's sacrifice.

Perhaps you have seen an electronic computer used to calculate mathematical problems. What happens if you get your information confused or make an error? You can press the "cancel" button and all of the information is eliminated. You can begin your calculation again without trying to sort out previous mistakes. The previous information is lost forever. That's what happens to your sins when God forgives you. The consequences often remain, but the guilt, the legal condemnation for the offense, is gone.

Because of the completeness of God's forgiveness you need never confess the same offense twice. Of course, if you commit the same sin again, you must confess it again to be restored to fellowship. But once a specific sin has been confessed to God, resolutely refuse to confess it again, even if guilt feelings should emerge.

I remember counseling a woman who lived with unresolved guilt because of premarital sexual experiences. Her guilt and subsequent unhappy marriage had cost her her health. I asked her if she had confessed her sins of the past. "Oh yes, I've confessed those sins a thousand times," she replied. "Well, has God forgiven you?" I asked. Her answer was, "I'm not sure."

What was this woman really saying? Quite unintentionally, she was denying that God had included her sin in Christ's death.

Why do people constantly reconfess the same sins? Sometimes, it's because they cannot believe that God would actually forgive so freely—surely they must suffer guilt first. Often they doubt whether they were sincere when they confessed their sins the first time. Or maybe they have never experienced grace and forgiveness from another person. Whatever the cause, Satan is winning a victory.

The Bible presents Satan as the accuser of the brethren, and when is he actively in business? During the night and during the day (see Rev. 12:10). He brings your sins before God and before you as well.

Satan delights in having believers reconfess the same sins. "Why don't you confess that sin again?" he suggests to your mind. The next day he tells you that you were insincere. "Confess that sin once more, but this time *really* mean business." And so it goes. You are trapped by your own unbelief and become the victim of your own emotions. The result: no love, joy, or peace. You miserably sit on the shelf labeled "Unsure of Forgiveness"—a shelf already populated by scores of spiritually paralyzed saints.

How do you avoid this trap? The secret is to *thank God for your forgiveness even when you still feel guilty.* Here's a suggestion: use your guilt feelings as a reminder to give praise to God for His forgiveness. Memorize Psalms 32 and 103 and recite them with thanksgiving to God when those guilt feelings surface. This will become a great stepping-stone in your life, for you will learn to walk by faith, not by emotional sight. And soon your feelings will catch up with your theology!

God promises you cleansing as well as forgiveness. First John 1:9 reads, "If we confess our sins, He is faithful and righteous to forgive us our sins and to cleanse us from all unrighteousness."

Forgiveness refers to your legal standing before God; cleansing is the subjective work of God whereby you are actually made clean.

A man freed from lust told me his story. Often he would ride a bus and be overcome with intense sexual desire. He confessed his sin, perhaps as often as two or three times a minute. But he discovered that, even after confession, his passions would continue. Rejecting sensual thoughts does not stop lustful desires that have been set in motion. But this man discovered the antidote to the problem. He insisted, not merely on God's forgiveness, but also on God's cleansing. "Sometimes I could feel the lust leave my body when I determined to accept God's cleansing." By receiving forgiveness and inner cleansing, you can put your past behind you.

3. Finally, as far as possible, experience the healing of all personal relationships. The severest guilt feelings usually attack when you have wronged others. You can accept your own hurt more easily than that of your family or friends. Here again, forgiveness is the only way to freedom. A telephone call or a casual meeting with that friend is often needed to satisfy your conscience. And what if he will not forgive you? If you have approached him in the right spirit, then be satisfied that you have done what you could to mend torn relationships.

Accepting God's Grace

God's grace is greater than your sin, whether the offense be big or small. A well-known Christian, driving too fast in the rain, caused an accident in which his companion was killed. Regret and wounds of guilt erupted in this man's heart. Yet he decided that he would not spend his whole life in the prison of self-incrimination. He chose to forgive himself, knowing that God had forgiven him. "That night," he says, "I saw more clearly than ever before that the purpose of the Cross is to repair the irreparable."

John Newton had godly parents but was orphaned at the age of six. He was adopted by a relative who rejected the boy's Christian heritage. At an early age, Newton became an apprentice seaman. While enlisted in the Royal Navy, he deserted and went to Africa for one purpose—to sin to his fill.

He became a servant to a wicked slave trader. Eventually, Newton escaped to the coast. There he attracted a ship by building a fire. Because he was a skilled navigator, he was soon made a mate on the vessel which was making its way up the coast of Africa to England.

On one occasion, he opened the casks of rum and distributed the liquor to the crew so that all the members became drunk. As the ship made its way to Great Britain, it was blown off course. When the ship began to flounder, Newton was sent into the hold to man the pumps along with the slaves who were being transported. The truth he had been taught as a child came home to him and he cried to God out of the hold of that ship. Later he wrote:

> Amazing grace! how sweet the sound,
> That saved a wretch like me!
> I once was lost, but now am found,
> Was blind, but now I see.

If God is able to forget your past, why can't you? He throws our sins into the depths of the sea and then puts up a sign on the shore which reads, "No fishing."

There is no reason for you to be trapped in the besmudged paths of your past life if God offers you a new beginning. Christ said to the woman taken in adultery, "Go, and sin no more." Once your past is forgiven, you are free from its grip. You are now at a fork in the road. With your sins forgiven, you can either return to the slippery slopes of failure or plant your feet on God's soil, and stand firmly on His side of the boundary line.

Suggested Application

1. Psalm 32 is an account of how David felt when he tried to hide his sin. List the effects of unconfessed sin mentioned in verses 3–5.

2. Think of actions for which we often feel guilty because we cannot forgive *ourselves*. How can we know whether our guilt is brought about by ourselves or by God?

3. Reread the account of the Fall in Genesis 3. What evidence is there that Adam and Eve felt guilty when God came to them? What characteristics of guilt are found in the record? What was God's response to their need?

4. Once we have confessed our sins, we must continually thank God for His pardon.

5. Memorize these verses and recite them as an expression of praise to God for His forgiveness: Psalm 32:1–2; Romans 8:33–34; 1 John 1:9.

4

GETTING GOD'S PERSPECTIVE

Are you still serious about breaking that sinful habit? Good. Let's get started. Since it is essential that you see your problem in perspective, let's look first at these four stories and try to put them in perspective.

• George, involved in an illicit sexual affair, told me that he had tried desperately to break this relationship. He had prayed to God for strength to overcome this liaison, earnestly pleading that his lust for this particular woman would evaporate. He was submerged in guilt, fear, and shame because he couldn't break the relationship. Eventually, the affair was discovered, he divorced his wife, and brought shame and hurt to both families.

• Ken was a truck driver who promised his wife he would quit smoking. He decided to decrease the number of cigarettes he smoked each day until he was free from the habit. He failed so many times that he gave up. Today, he is convinced he can never quit and has no intention of trying.

• Mary was overweight. The doctor assured her that the cause was not a physical problem, but was due to her overeating. She tried several diets over a period of months. This wasn't easy for her; she unrealistically expected dramatic and immediate results. Repeatedly, she broke her promises to herself. Eventually, discouragement turned to hopelessness, and Mary gave up trying to lose weight.

• John was a man with an explosive temper. Sharp words shot out of his mouth, shattering his wife's self-confidence and affection. He overdisciplined his children, usually in a fit of anger. As a Christian, he knew better and even decided to change. Once, after a particularly sharp exchange with his wife, he put his fist through the wall. Humiliated and guilt-ridden, he asked God for deliverance from his temper. Vowing to change did not help; neither did his praying. Months later he gave up, saying, "I can't help myself. That's just the way I am."

What went wrong? All of these people were Christians, all prayed to be delivered, yet all ended up more discouraged than when they began. The easy answer is to say, "They weren't sincere—if they'd have meant it, God would have helped them." However, I believe they were sincere in their praying, in some cases they even wept. Apparently, sincerity in itself doesn't guarantee deliverance.

One reason why these people reverted back to their old behavior patterns is that *they misunderstood the full extent of their problem*. True, they wanted victory, but they didn't understand how or why God would bring it about. They, like most of us, wanted to overcome a specific habit—for their own benefit. They wanted to be free of the symptoms of their problem, but did not want a thorough examination that would reveal deeper problems in their lives which they were unwilling to face. The habits themselves were like the tip of an iceberg. Let me explain.

• George wanted to break his adulterous relationship because he felt guilty; furthermore, he lived in constant fear of being discovered. He sought God's assistance to save his marriage and, above all, his reputation. This, of course, is understandable; we can all identify with such motivation. But his life needed many other adjustments.

To begin with, his marriage was in disarray before the affair began. He had a hot temper and had begun to deeply wound his wife's spirit soon after their marriage. His proud, self-righteous spirit had strained his relationship with his two children. He was selfish, spending his free time fixing race cars. His family was considered an inconvenience.

What was God's concern for this man? That he stop his adulterous relationship? Yes. But much more besides. God wanted him to humble himself, to ask the forgiveness of his wife and children, to reorganize his priorities. Attitudes had to be confessed, pride had to be broken, and selfishness had to be faced head-on. More importantly, God desired to become Number One in his life. But George wasn't concerned about such drastic treatment. God wanted to give him a whole housecleaning, but George wanted only the dirt swept from his front steps.

• And what about Ken? He wanted to quit smoking. Yes, he was a Christian, but lived only on the fringes of spiritual commitment. His children had never heard him pray, except for the perfunctory grace said at mealtimes. He was not a spiritual leader in his home; his wife taught the children the few Bible stories they knew.

Now he wanted God to help him quit smoking because the doctors told him he might die of lung cancer. Could God help him overcome that habit? Yes indeed. But he would have to yield himself fully to God—his time, property, and reputation would have to be committed to the Almighty. Ken would have to begin reading the Scriptures and turning to God daily for the needs of himself and his family. But he didn't bargain for such changes. He thought God would deliver him from cigarettes and leave the rest of his life untouched.

• Then there is Mary. Yes, she desperately wanted to lose those ugly pounds. But she did not see her problem as a genuinely spiritual one. She spoke of it as her weakness, without treating it as a sin of the flesh. The Bible condemns gluttony (Deut. 21:20; 1 Peter 4:3). The writer of Proverbs warns that "the heavy drinker and the glutton will come to poverty" (Prov. 23:21). Paul even wept over those whose god was their appetite (Phil. 3:19). Those who struggle with gluttony must renew their mind, and use the Scriptures to resist Satan just as anyone who is caught in the other sins of sensuality.

Undoubtedly, God wanted to use Mary's problem to teach her valuable lessons about resisting temptation, the tactics of Satan, and above all, the remarkable power of the Word of God. But sadly, her mind was focused only on her weight. She passed up an opportunity to take some giant steps in her Christian life.

• Finally, there is John. His problem, so he thought, was that he was born with a short fuse. And of course, his circumstances were to blame—if everything would go more to his liking, there would be no need to blow up, no need to put his fist through the wall. One reason John still lacks self-control today is because of his unwillingness to face his underlying attitude toward God and his family. Actually, John is always angry—angry at his employer, angry at life itself. He feels he has been gypped because he has never been the success his father hoped he'd be. Though he doesn't realize it, he is a man at war with God, rebelling against the vocation and circumstances of life to which God has called him. Until he accepts himself and his place in the world with joyful thanksgiving, he will never learn to control his temper. God is concerned about changing these attitudes, but John isn't. He wants victory over his temper to avoid future embarrassment and to keep his marriage intact. He wants the minimum required to maintain his life on a fairly even keel—but no more than this.

Face the Issues

How easily we want freedom from a particular sin without facing basic issues! One day, a man who had been fired from his job called me on the phone. I had never met him, but he asked me what he could do to develop his willpower. He simply could not get to work on time and had been fired from two previous jobs because of his laziness. I gave him some suggestions, hoping to help him.

A week later, I received a phone call from a woman asking advice on how to break up an illicit sexual affair. To my chagrin, the man involved was the one I had spoken to a week before! His problem of sensuality had affected all areas of his life. How accurate James was when he taught that a double-minded man is unstable in *all* his ways (James 1:8).

Sinful habits are usually indicative of unresolved conflicts. We must always seek underlying causes rather than treating the symptoms. God uses our struggles with sin to diagnose our true condition. Temptation is His X-ray machine, discovering the hidden conflicts that need attention.

What Does God Want to Accomplish?

God has a larger purpose in wanting to show us our inner self. Unfortunately, we too often clutch the smaller purpose: we desire freedom from sin to avoid embarrassment, be relieved of guilt, or to save a marriage. However, the deeper issue we often avoid is our rebellion against God. A man may be dishonest in business; a woman may have had an abortion—both want to be free from a nagging conscience, but they may not be willing to deal with their basic attitude of defiance of God's authority.

Genuine repentance is never easy. To confess your sins means that you agree with God that you have sinned; it also means that you agree that the sin must be forsaken. Those who confess their sins, intending to repeat the same action, are only partially repentant. Such incomplete repentance leads to a downward spiral of repeated failure. Confession means that you admit your sin and give God permission to remove it from your life. Of course, I'm not saying that you will never commit the same sin again—if so, none of us could claim forgiveness. But there needs to be willingness to part with the sin, and a submission to God's verdict on the matter. Apart from such an acknowledgment, your intentions are self-centered. You are inquiring how forgiveness will benefit you instead of considering how you have offended God.

But don't stop here. God wants to draw you beyond your repentance for sin to Himself. He wants to use your struggles to lead you into godly living. His will is not merely that you be free from sin; He wants to conform you to the image of His Son. Delivering you from sinful habits is only a step in the process. Washing the stains from your life is His prelude to changing you into the Spirit-filled person God wants you to be.

A young man, caught in the grip of homosexuality, struggled with this sin for a period of months. God eventually changed him so radically that he developed normal attractions for the opposite sex. Today he is a godly, sensitive young man. God taught him principles of commitment which he has been able to apply to all areas of his life. He memorized more than two hundred verses of Scripture during those months of agonizing struggle. His sinful habit drove him to seek God and become intimately acquainted with the Almighty. He began by being occupied with his problem; today he is occupied with his God.

When you are faced with excruciating temptation, you have a choice to make. You can say: "I've tried to change before and it hasn't worked, so I'll manage the best I can with my sin. We're all human, you know." Your sin will be a monument to the false god you have fashioned.

Or, you can take a look at your sinful habit and see it as a challenge to display God's grace and power in your life. To the scattered Jewish Christians, James wrote, "Consider it all joy, my brethren, when you encounter various trials, knowing that the testing of your faith produces endurance. And let endurance have its perfect result, that you may be perfect and complete, lacking in nothing" (James 1:2–4).

God does not pass out packages of spiritual victory sent Special Delivery to the person who requests them. Your sin cost Him the death of His Son; He is not about to hand out spiritual bandages. He uses your struggles to give you a thorough housecleaning, reorganize your priorities and make you dependent on His grace. There are no cheap, easy miracles. You must want spiritual freedom, not merely for your own sake, but for God's sake as well. Only then will you find the victory He promises.

Getting a Larger Focus

There is quite a difference between temptation and sin. Choosing to pursue the temptation is sin but the temptation itself isn't. Even our Lord was tempted.

When sinful thoughts enter your mind, unwelcomed and without fanfare, at that point you have not sinned. Now the crucial test comes: how will you respond to these suggestions? Will you pursue these thoughts, entertain them, and let them be at home in your mind?

Many Christians think that victory over sin means that they will no longer be tempted. Or they think that God will change their nature so that they will no longer desire to do evil. Either way, they are wrong. Temptation is not a sin: it is a call to battle.

I remember my own struggles with sinful lusts, as I implored God to deliver me from these passions. I expected God to change my desires so that I would no longer be stimulated when temptations came my way. Needless to say, I was disappointed.

God does not change our nature so that we are less than human. Temptation of one kind or another is universal. To pray that we will no longer be tempted is to ask that we die and go to heaven. Since we will always be tempted, we need to learn to handle temptation in God's way.

1. As you think of that sin you want to overcome, first thank God for this temptation and the opportunity it represents in your life. Don't thank God for the sin, thank Him for the temptation which gives you a clear-cut opportunity to declare your allegiance to Jesus Christ. Praise, persistent praise, is the first positive step toward overcoming temptation. God is glorified when you accept your circumstances as from His hand. If you cannot thank God for your condition and even your temptation, you are rebelling against Him. One man wrestling with a fierce temptation told me he could not resist it until he gave thanks to God continually for his struggle. "Lord," he prayed, "I thank You for this temptation; even if I should be tempted from now until the day I die, I give thanks for it."

The first step in getting God's perspective? Accept the fact that you will be tempted; then choose to thank God for the opportunity it represents.

2. Take a tour through your life, jotting down areas that need work. Spend some time defining your basic attitudes. What is it that *really* bothers you? What do you really want? Are you rebelling against some person? Are you upset with your performance? your appearance? Do you feel like a failure, a big zero? Do you think that you have been shortchanged since becoming a Christian? Are you bitter against your parents, children, husband, or wife? Are you angry at God because He hasn't done what you think He ought? Spend an unhurried hour taking inventory.

Whenever I've done this, I've discovered attitudes I didn't know I had. For example, I'm often upset with myself because it takes me so long to accomplish a project—writing a book, for instance. I've uncovered dissatisfaction with my job, lingering regret over failures at the university (I failed a comprehensive exam last fall), and frustration in personal relationships. All of this affects my attitude, my perspective. God has been showing me that the way I handle these attitudes will affect my relationship to Him, and will bring honor or dishonor to my heavenly Father.

3. After you have had time to reflect on your private struggles, give yourself and your problem completely to God. This means that you let go of it, no longer claiming your right of control—or your right to bitterness. Do so, knowing that God will require you to deal with those attitudes you have uncovered. This may be a painful and long process, but it will be lastingly beneficial.

Don't be afraid of what God might demand of you. One woman who was very shy and withdrawn told me she was afraid to give herself to God, because she might have to learn to be friendly.

You can be sure that God will not demand more from you than you can do. Whatever God asks of you, He will give you the strength to do.

When you come to a stream where the bridge has washed away, it still may be possible to cross it—not in short steps, but with one long jump. So it is when we give ourselves to God. When the bridge of blame and excuses is gone, take that one long leap, without any thought of returning to a life of halfhearted commitment. Though your dedication may have to be renewed many times, make it as clear, specific, and final as you can, knowing God will be with you to keep you walking in His way.

4. Realize that your ultimate goal is not victory, but God Himself. Augustine wrote in his *Confessions,* "O Lord, thou hast made us for Thyself, and our hearts are restless until they find their all in Thee." Ultimately, not even victory over sin can satisfy. Only God can do that, for He has made you to need person-to-person relationships. And He is the Person in whose likeness we are made.

Remember Copernicus? He was the astronomer who concluded that the earth rotated around the sun, and not vice versa. With the sun at the center of the universe, the planetary motion could be explained more easily. The complicated equations needed to explain the movement of planets were simplified by this new theory.

God wants you to have your own Copernican revolution. He longs to be brought from the circumference to the very center of your life to make your life meaningful and rewarding and to give you the beautiful simplicity of life that serves a sovereign who is both Creator and Redeemer. The victory over sin that you seek will come from your relationship with God. When you seek to know God and love Him with your whole mind, heart, and soul, the freedom you are looking for will become yours.

You may think that knowing God is a rather theoretical and mystical goal. God is invisible, and may seem inaccessible. Isn't it easier to establish goals in business or in your marriage and family life?

The wonderful promise of the Scriptures is that you *can* know God. To the prophet Jeremiah, God said, "You will call upon Me and come and pray to Me, and I will listen to you. And you will seek Me and find Me, when you search for Me with all your heart. And I will be found by you" (Jer. 29:12–14).

Throughout the Bible, the desire to know God is compared to a thirst. The Old Testament prophets spoke of the time when the land would be flowing with water, when God Himself would give His people springs in the desert.

Jesus spoke of Himself as the One who could give the living water. "If any man is thirsty, let him come to Me and drink. He who believes in Me, as the Scriptures said, 'From his innermost being shall flow rivers of living water' " (John 7:37–38).

Are you thirsty for this living, lasting water, this satisfaction in your innermost self? This poem by Nancy Spiegelberg may describe your experience.

> Lord,
> I crawled
> across the barrenness
> to You
> with my empty cup,
>
> uncertain
> but asking
> any small drop
> of refreshment.
>
> If only
> I had known You better
> I'd have come
> running with a bucket.
> (*Decision*, November 1974)

The better you know God, the more often you turn to Him. The more you understand that you are created for fellowship with Him, the more time you will spend fulfilling that purpose, until your life demonstrates the singleness of devotion that Paul expressed: "This one thing I do."

Seeing with God's perspective means that you will learn to pray optimistically and in faith. God has brought this temptation to you for your good. Now thank Him for how He will use it. He wants to build and not to destroy. If He wounds you, it is so that He might heal you in the depths of your being.

If you are serious about breaking that sinful habit, why not pray right now, thanking God for what He will do in your life?

Lord, I confess my sin, particularly my rebellion against Your authority. In agreeing that I have sinned, I also agree that this sin must be forsaken. Thank You for Your forgiveness.

I am grateful for this powerful temptation which gives me the chance to prove that I love You more than any pleasure in the world. I thank You that the temptation is not greater than I can bear, and I rejoice at how You will use it in my life.

I look forward to getting to know You better, and I am glad that You have sent me this trial as a reminder of how desperately I need You. Help me to remember to give thanks at all times and in all circumstances.

In Jesus' Name,
Amen.

Suggested Application

1. Most of our repeated failures stem from one of three basic causes (a) pride, (b) sensuality, and (c) covetousness. Read Genesis 3:1–8 and try to find these three elements in Satan's temptation of Adam and Eve.

2. Try to relate your particular temptation to one or more of the root problems mentioned above. For example: the sin of anger actually reflects pride. We become upset when circumstances do not conform to what we would like. We lose control of ourselves when we cannot control situations according to our own desires.

3. Think of some Bible characters who tried to cover or excuse their sin. What was the result for them personally, and for other people?

4. Take Paul's list of the works of the flesh in Galatians 5:19–21, and describe the way in which each one is symptomatic of rebellion against God.

5. In thinking of the particular sin you would like to overcome, ask: what would God want to *put in the place of* this habit? Read the Beatitudes and find the character qualities that seem to be directly opposite to the trait you want God to change (Matt. 5:1–10).

5

THE FREEDOM OF LIVING AT THE CROSS

The chains of habit are so light you cannot feel them, until they are so strong you cannot break them. Sin does not appear to be irresistible—until you want to be free from it. The moment you attack it, you are surprised to find that most of its power is hidden. You feel like the man who tried to drain a swamp, not knowing it was fed by an underground stream.

Let's take gluttony as an example. Mary thought for sure she would be able to control her diet whenever she wanted to. But here's what happened: after gaining a few unnecessary pounds she felt guilty. Her response to this uncomfortable emotion was to promise herself that she would stick to her diet. *Never* would she overeat again, *never*! But she was disgusted with herself when she did not keep her promise. Guilt drove her to more promises, and her self-condemnation increased. At last, Mary gave up.

How vividly I recall just such an experience. I promised myself (vowed would be a better word) that I would never say yes to a particular temptation. But the next time I faced it, I gave in once more. What was even more shocking was that I said *yes* to this temptation even when I felt like saying *no*! At that point I gave up making promises, knowing I'd never keep them anyway.

Since then I've discovered that promises to reform are not only worthless, but even detrimental in changing our behavior. One reason is because we are depending on our own strength to change. Even when we ask God to help us keep that promise, we have as yet not grasped the extent of our weakness. Also, such resolutions divert our attention to the wrong focus. We spend time looking within ourselves wondering (usually doubting) whether we really have the inner resources to remain firm. All the while we're looking in the wrong direction.

Let's assume that you've confessed your sin to God; you've repented, admitting that all sin is rebellion against Him. What then? You must choose to focus your attention on God's promises. Tell the Lord you are through with *your* promises, and are now depending on *His* promises. You are tired of the guilt-sin-guilt cycle. You finally admit that He alone ". . . is able to keep you from stumbling, and to make you stand in the presence of His glory blameless with great joy" (Jude 24). *If you make a promise, let it be a promise to meditate on God's Word.*

Now your attention will no longer be occupied with the question of whether you have the willpower to say no to that particular temptation; your thoughts will be on the Scriptures. This in itself will be a help since we tend to do the activities we think about the most—that's why we do so many things we plan to resist! But when we are free from the pressure of wondering whether we can hold out, our minds are able to soak up the Scriptures and focus on Christ.

Also, you'll discover that the Holy Spirit will give you the ability to say *no*, when the temptation comes. In other words, it's up to the Holy Spirit to free you from the compulsion to repeat your sinful behavior.

This is not a once-for-all decision. It usually begins at a definite point—we finally come to the end of our resolutions and throw ourselves helplessly before a merciful God. That is the beginning, but it is not the end.

The fact that I've come to trust God to keep me from stumbling, is not a guarantee that I'll never fall. It just means that *while I am trusting Him,* I am opening my life to His help. As long as I say *yes* to God, I will be saying *no* to temptation.

Saying *yes* means that I must choose to focus on the Cross. By understanding my identification with Christ, I will learn that God is indeed able to keep me from sinning. In fact, God will not only drain the swamp, but stop the underground supply.

Finding the Source

Did you know that all sinful habits have a common source? There is a tendency to think of some sins as "less" sinful than others. You may say to yourself, "I have a bad temper, but at least I don't drink" or "I do struggle with overeating, but I'd never have an affair."

It is true that some sins do have worse *consequences* than others. The *thoughts* of lust and hatred do not lead to the same social consequences as the *acts* of adultery and murder. In this sense all sins are not the same. But from another perspective, all sins are essentially the same because they originate from the same source. We can't rate sins on a scale somewhere between Serious and Minor. Some sins may seem unimportant to us, but they are not to God. The reason: all sins originate from the corruption of our rebellious sinful nature. The New Testament writers often referred to this as "the flesh," a compulsive inner force inherited from man's fall which expresses itself in general and specific rebellion against God. (Mark Bubeck, *The Adversary*. Chicago: Moody Press, 1975, p. 28.)

Read these verses carefully to find your particular sinful habit listed, "Now the deeds of the flesh are evident, which are: immorality, impurity, sensuality, idolatry, sorcery, enmities, strife, jealousy, outbursts of anger, disputes, dissensions, factions, envying, drunkenness, carousing and things like these'' (Gal. 5:19–21a).

All of these behavioral patterns sprout from the same seed—the flesh. We cannot console ourselves by saying that we have one sin, but not another. The flesh is a tree with different kinds of branches bearing many kinds of sin. In me, it might produce outbursts of anger; in you, it might express itself in sorcery, or perhaps gluttony. But both of us, though diverse in behavior and temperament, are controlled by the flesh. That's why self-righteousness, which always involves a spirit of comparison, is so abhorrent to God. It thrives on a superficial view of sin (mine are not as bad as yours), and an equally superficial view of God (surely I'm within reach of His standards).

The Bible puts an end to such vanity. *All* have sinned; *all* by nature fulfill the desires of the flesh and of the mind. You may think your sin is minor, but it needs the same drastic treatment as that of a criminal whose whole life has been twisted by perversion. Your flesh and his are essentially the same; he may not have had your advantages, or perhaps God's grace has restrained you.

If this sounds discouraging to those who think their sinful habit is of little importance, it ought to be *encouraging* to those who see themselves as beyond hope. Your sinful pattern is no different *in principle* from that of any other person. Some habits are more ingrained than others, but God's remedy for each is the same.

The flesh or the self is so much a part of our thinking that we often do not even recognize its presence. Just in case you still think that you may have escaped its influence, here are some questions to ask yourself.

Are you ever conscious of:

- A secret spirit of pride; an exalted feeling in view of your success of position, because of your good training and appearance, because of your natural gifts and abilities; an important independent spirit; stiffness and preciseness.

- The stirrings of anger or impatience, which, worst of all, you call nervousness or holy indignation; a touchy, sensitive spirit; a disposition which dislikes being contradicted; a desire to throw sharp, heated words at another.
- Self-will; a stubborn, unteachable spirit; an arguing, talkative spirit; harsh, sarcastic expressions; an unyielding, headstrong disposition; a driving, commanding spirit; a disposition to criticize and pick flaws when set aside and unnoticed; a peevish, fretful spirit; a disposition that loves to be coaxed and humored.
- Carnal fear; a man-fearing spirit; a shrinking from reproach and duty; reasoning around your cross; a shrinking from doing your whole duty by those of wealth or position; a fearfulness that someone will offend and drive some prominent person away; a compromising spirit.
- A jealous disposition; a secret spirit of envy shut up in your heart; an unpleasant sensation in view of the great prosperity and success of another; a disposition to speak of the faults and failings rather than the gifts and virtues of those more talented and appreciated than yourself.
- A dishonest, deceitful disposition; the evading and covering of the truth; the covering up of your real faults; the leaving of a better impression of yourself than is strictly true; false humility; exaggeration; straining the truth.
- Unbelief; a spirit of discouragement in times of pressure; lack of faith and trust in God; a disposition to worry and complain in the midst of pain, poverty, or at the dispensations of Divine Providence; an over anxious feeling about whether everything will come out all right.
- Formality and deadness, lack of concern for lost souls; dryness and indifference; lack of power with God. ("Traits of the Self-Life." Saskatoon, Saskatchewan, Canada: Western Tract Missions.)

God's Solution

Fortunately, God chose to become involved in our predicament. The death of His Son was a solution designed to free us from the frustration of nonfulfillment. We momentarily enjoy the works of the flesh, but later hate ourselves for what we have done. We resolve to change, yet later crave the same old sins.

Christ's death accomplished many objectives. The Cross is the basis for your forgiveness. It is also the basis for your spiritual freedom—deliverance from your stubborn habits. To appreciate what Christ did, you should become acquainted with two expressions: *in Adam* and *in Christ*.

When Adam sinned, the whole human race was plunged into chaos. His descendants have never recovered from that debacle. Your sin nature was inherited from your parents, grandparents, and great-grandparents; your ancestry can be traced back to the Garden of Eden. As a result, you are a sinner by nature and already under sin's condemnation. Being *in Adam* means you are victimized by sin, and quite literally cannot help yourself—you sin as naturally as birds sprout feathers.

But because of Christ's death, believers are transferred from being in Adam to being *in Christ*. God breaks your past ties and Christ becomes your new ancestor, spiritually speaking. That's why Paul refers more than 100 times to believers as being "in Christ." It's the basis for a whole new life.

All of this seems rather theoretical. Is there some value to this transfer of relationship? After all, when you were converted, you still looked the same, felt the same, and (unfortunately) often acted the same. On the surface, it sounds like being "in Christ" or "in Adam" is only a matter of words.

Not so. Think of a child who is adopted from one family to another. The fact of adoption doesn't change his appearance or his actions. But if he is taken from a family of slaves and adopted into a family of kings, he inherits a new set of relationships. "Therefore if any man is in Christ, he is a new creature; the old things passed away; behold, new things have come" (2 Cor. 5:17).

Here's what happens: God identifies all believers with Christ, not in some mystical or theoretical way, but by changing our legal relationships. Before our conversion, we were obligated to obey the sinful impulses of our fallen race. Even when we became tired of sin and resolved to change, the most we could do was rearrange our lives, but we could not change on the inside.

God has done what we could not do. He has given us a new nature, and the personal presence and power of the Holy Spirit so that we can say *No* to our old self-nature.

To picture what God has done, think of yourself as a tenant in an apartment house. The landlord is making your life miserable and charges exorbitant rent. He mistreats you, barges into your apartment, wrecks the furniture, and then blames *you* for it. One day a new owner buys the apartment complex. You now have a kind landlord who invites you to live in the apartment rent-free. You are relieved, grateful, and looking forward to a peaceful future.

A few hours later there is a knock on the door. To your amazement, here is your old landlord, looking as mean and demanding as ever. He threatens you, reminding you that you have rented from him for many years and are obligated to obey him.

What will you do? To resist him on your own is useless—he's more powerful than you are. Your best approach is to remind him you are now under a different management; he'll have to take up your case with the new landlord (Larry Christenson, *The Renewed Mind*. Minneapolis: Bethany Fellowship, 1974, pp. 41–42).

How much obligation do you have to your old landlord? Precisely as much as does a corpse buried in the cemetery down the street. Your former landlord has no more right to demand a payment from you than he does from those whose names appear in the obituary column. That's why Paul exhorted us, "Even so consider yourselves to be dead to sin, but alive to God in Christ Jesus"

(Rom. 6:11). Your authority to say *No* to temptation is God-given.

Although before our conversion we were duty-bound to serve our inherited sin nature, this does not mean that everything we did was evil. Most people are able to control their desires, and are capable of compassion and decency.

What it does mean is that we were never free from the futility of unsatisfied desires and frustrated passions. Pride, covetousness, and sensuality were our motivational drives. As believers purchased by Christ at high cost, our allegiance is now to Him. By the Holy Spirit, He has given us the power to say Yes to a new life.

Where the Rubber Meets the Road

How do you apply this knowledge when you want to break a specific habit? First, you must clearly see that legally in Christ you *are already dead* to your sinful passions. This is a point many people resist. They think, "I've got to *become dead*; I've got to pray that God will *crucify me* so that I will be alive in Christ." But they are wrong. Being dead to sin is not something which God promises you; it is not an act you beg Him to do. He simply declares it as a *fact*—already accomplished. Your failures and sins cannot change what God has said. Just because you get talked into obeying your old landlord doesn't change the fact of new management. It does mean that you forgot you could confidently say *No* to his extortion schemes.

Let's say, for example, that you are a believer who lives with fear—perhaps a fear of people, cancer, or loneliness. Then recognize those fears as a bill from your old landlord. Remember that you do not have to listen to him—much less do what he suggests. Take the matter up with your new Manager. You are no longer duty-bound to those former relationships.

Second, you must admit the *need for faith* in your daily life. Your identification with Christ is not something which can be proved empirically; it's not like being able to see with your own eyes that the sun is shining. And even if it could be proven by our experience, many of us would be in trouble. An honest look at our lives hardly supports the idea that we are dead to sin and alive to God. But once we understand, with the Holy Spirit's help, that our ties with sin have *already* been broken, we begin to see that God has not deceived us. When we shift our attention to the completed work of the Cross and insist on our privileges, our old self surrenders to God's authority. Through faith and faith alone we personalize our victory.

Let me add that your freedom from sin is never automatic. Every inch is contested. No one ever falls into maturity, even though you are already positionally complete in Christ. One danger of reading a book like this is that you may tend to look for formulas for a new spiritual technique. But there is no substitute for waiting before God, reading His Word, and then obeying the truth He has revealed.

The Christian life is a growing relationship. Applying the Cross to your life is not something you do once for all. Nor is it sufficient to do it every week or even once a day. It is a moment by moment, daily process. As you develop sensitivity to the Holy Spirit's work in your life, you will find that saying *No* to the flesh and *Yes* to Christ will become a way of life. In the next chapter, you will learn how to personalize Christ's victory.

Suggested Application

1. If you have not already done so, now is the time to take stock of your life, asking: what behavior patterns or thoughts must be changed by God?

2. Read Romans, chapters 6—8, carefully underlining each time Paul uses the expression "free from sin" or its equivalent. In each case, find what Paul gives as a basis for your freedom.

3. The more clearly we see the wide-ranging benefits of the Cross, the more we will develop a life of habitual praise. Begin this habit by thanking God three times a day for the victory Christ accomplished on your behalf.

4. Begin each day at the Cross. Take time to:
   a. give thanks that Christ has *already* conquered the problems you will face that day
   b. accept by faith the victory Christ won at the cross— *before* you are tempted to sin.

6

THE POWER OF THE HOLY SPIRIT

Years ago when slavery was officially abolished in Jamaica, some of the slaves in the remote areas did not know of their freedom. Years after their release had been announced they still continued to serve their masters, oblivious to the fact that they were legally free. Their owners kept the news from the slaves as long as possible, hoping to extract every ounce of work from their captives. The slaves wouldn't have had to put up with their drudgery—except for their ignorance of the facts.

Jesus Christ issues a proclamation of liberty to every believer. We've already learned that our union with Him qualifies us to share His victory. But precisely how is His victory translated into our experience? The answer lies in the personal ministry of the Holy Spirit. He communicates Christ's strength to us; He satisfies our spiritual thirst. Let's consider what Christ had to say about the Spirit's ministry.

When Jesus Christ attended the Feast of Tabernacles at Jerusalem, He was deeply moved by the emptiness of the ritual the Jews dutifully performed. On that day, a group of white-robed priests went down to the pool of Siloam. They filled their jars with water from the pool and then walked home to the temple and poured out the water in the presence of the people. This was to remind them of how God supplied Israel's need for water during their wandering in the wilderness.

This ceremony was a beautiful reminder of what God had done, but the people missed its spiritual meaning—that God wanted to satisfy their spiritual thirst as well. The Scripture says, "On the last day of the feast, He (Jesus) stood and cried out saying, 'If any man is thirsty, let him come to Me and drink. He who believes in Me, as the Scripture said, "From his innermost being shall flow rivers of living water." ' But this He spoke of the Spirit, whom those who believe in Him were to receive; for the Spirit was not yet given, because Jesus was not yet glorified" (John 7:37–39). Here, Christ predicted the coming of the new age when the Holy Spirit would be poured out upon His people.

Notice carefully that the basis of the gift of the Spirit is the *glorification* of Jesus Christ. The Spirit, Jesus said, could not be given to His people until He was glorified. God doesn't give the Spirit because you agonize for Him or fast; rather, it's because Jesus has ascended into heaven. In the Old Testament era, the Spirit's work was limited; after Christ's ascension, the Spirit was given to every believer.

Listen to the words of Christ: "But I tell you the truth, it is to your advantage that I go away; for if I do not go away, the Helper shall not come to you; but if I go, I will send Him to you" (John 16:7). Christ could not give the Spirit to the church until He left this earth physically. He had to be glorified before the Spirit could descend upon His people.

Think of it this way. Jesus Christ's death on the cross is the basis for your forgiveness. Because He took your penalty, you can receive forgiveness of sins without strings attached; the only requirement is trust—a transfer of your faith from yourself to Christ alone. Similarly, the basis on which the Holy Spirit is given is Christ's ascension and glorification. You don't have to beg for forgiveness, nor do you need to agonize for the Spirit; the water of life is also free, and is received by faith.

Ever since Christ was glorified, and the Spirit was given on the Day of Pentecost, every believer has received Him (Rom. 8:9; 1 Cor. 6:19). There is no need for striving, anxiety, or a feeling that we are unworthy to receive Him. He is waiting to quench our thirst, but His control in our lives is never automatic.

How Do We Receive the Spirit's Power?

Do you know the reaction of many Christians when you talk to them about the fullness of the Spirit? They say, "That's great for others, but I'm not good enough. I don't qualify. If I were more dedicated and spent more time in Bible reading and prayer, I might eventually be worthy to walk in the Spirit."

But we've got it backwards. The Holy Spirit is not given to those who have it all together spiritually; *He is given to enable us to get it together spiritually!* I'm struck with Paul's words: "But I say, walk by the Spirit and you will not carry out the desire of the flesh" (Gal. 5:16). Notice the sequence. Paul does *not* say that if we stop carrying out the desires of the flesh we will walk in the Spirit; *rather,* if we walk in the Spirit, we will not fulfill the desires of the flesh!

That order makes an incredible difference. Christians often ignore any thought of walking by the Spirit, because they think they are not good enough. Their life is too filled with fleshly struggles. But that's like refusing to accept medicine until you get well and feel worthy of it!

The whole purpose of medicine is to enable you to get well. It is given to the sick, not the healthy. In the same way, the Spirit is given to enable you to break sin's power; you don't have to do that on your own before you receive the Spirit's power.

Imagine someone saying, "I'm not good enough to be saved; I'm going to wait until I get myself together before I come to

Christ.'' You would quickly point out that salvation is designed for sinners. None of us is ever good enough to be saved; we are saved because of God's great generosity in Christ. A person who says he isn't good enough is missing the point of Christ's death.

But the same applies to the Holy Spirit. As Christ's death gives us forgiveness, so Christ's ascension and glorification give us the Holy Spirit. And the coming of the Holy Spirit into our lives is not just for window dressing. *He indwells us so that He might control us.*

I believe that we have often made the requirements for walking in the Spirit too complicated. We've stressed dedication, surrender, and discipline as prerequisites to the Spirit's power. When I read books that give seven steps to the filling of the Spirit or others that condense it to four, I find myself asking, Can any one of us be sure we have *fully* carried out all of these requirements? Is not the Spirit's power given to sinners to enable them to be yielded and disciplined, rather than expecting all of these characteristics from them first?

Notice Christ's words: "If any man is thirsty, let him come unto Me and drink." The only requirement is a thirst that will draw you to come to Him. We don't have to be supersaints, just thirsty sinners. That's why Christ could offer living water to a woman who had had five husbands and was now living common-law. He promised that from within her would burst forth living water that would quench her emotional and spiritual thirst (John 4:10–14).

Are you thirsty? Do you feel, as I have often felt, like an apple tree trying to grow in a desert? Then you are a candidate for the Spirit's life and power.

Life in the Spirit

There is a direct connection between walking in the Spirit and breaking a sinful habit. Today, many people suffer from drug addiction. Perhaps they began getting high just for kicks, but now they are hooked. In New Testament times, drugs as we know them today were not available. But many became addicted to wine. Speaking to that issue, Paul wrote, "And do not get drunk with wine, for that is dissipation, but be filled with the Spirit" (Eph. 5:18). To those who are struggling with addiction of any kind, the Bible offers a different master: be controlled by the Spirit, rather than drugs or alcohol or any other stubborn habit. The Spirit's control will replace sin's control. His power is greater than the power of all your sin.

Well, here you stand, weighted down with a sin you can't shrug off. It hangs on you like a viper; if it leaves you alone for one day, it is back the next. I bet you're saying, "OK, Lutzer. How do I get the Holy Spirit's help?"

You begin by clearing the deck—confessing your sin and the sin must be confessed—and receiving God's forgiveness. Claim 1 John 1:9, "If we confess our sins, He is faithful and righteous to forgive us our sins and to cleanse us from all unrighteousness."

Then, remember that the Holy Spirit desires to energize you. Don't ever think that He is reluctant, wanting to be coaxed into the driver's seat of your life. *He became a resident with the express purpose of becoming president.* But He will not exercise His power apart from your faith. If you ask Him to control you, believe that He will.

Maybe you feel unworthy, or think that there will be a more convenient time. F.B. Meyer tells of his experience: "I left the prayer meeting and crept away into the lane praying, 'O Lord, if there was ever a man who needs the power of the Holy Spirit, it is I. But I do not know how to receive Him, I am too tired, too worn, too nervously run down to agonize.' Then a voice said to me, 'As you took forgiveness from the hand of the dying Christ, take the Holy Spirit from the hand of the living Christ.' " Meyer goes on to say, "I took for the first time and have kept on taking ever since."

How were you saved? By depending on the death of Christ. How do you receive the power of the Spirit? By depending on the ascension of Christ. Both come by faith. That's why Paul wrote, "As you therefore have received Christ Jesus the Lord, so walk in Him" (Col. 2:6).

You receive the Spirit's filling by faith, not by having a particular feeling. Some Christians wrongly believe that the filling of the Spirit is a sensation. They expect waves of love, or an overwhelming sense of peace, or speaking in strange languages. Theirs is a fleshly desire to walk by sight, not by faith. We find it difficult to take God at His Word, and like the Pharisees, we ask for a sign that we might believe.

God, however, delights when you believe in Him without demanding emotional crutches. Just as a new believer needs to receive God's promises—apart from feelings—so you daily need to receive the power of the Holy Spirit—apart from feelings.

Living by Praise

You will be greatly helped in accepting the Spirit's control if you learn the power of praise. "He who offers a sacrifice of thanksgiving honors Me; and to him who orders his way aright I shall show the salvation of God" (Ps. 50:23). Paul put it this way: "In everything give thanks; for this is God's will for you in Christ Jesus" (1 Thes. 5:18).

When you read these exhortations to praise, you may make two very common errors. One is to think you should praise God only for the good things He gives you—health, food, clothes, and other blessings. The second is to think that you should praise God only when you *feel* like doing so. But Paul wrote, "In *everything* give thanks." That means *all* circumstances, whether pleasant or painful.

I find it extremely difficult to give thanks to God when I fail an exam or on a day when everything goes wrong. But it's only when we choose to give praise for the rough spots in life that we will begin to see them from God's perspective. Furthermore, if we don't give thanks in all things, we are living in unbelief, for we are assuming that our circumstances are not controlled by a God who loves us! I'm not saying that you should give thanks for sin, but you can thank God for how He will *use* that sin to teach, to rebuke, or to challenge you.

Also, you can learn to give thanks even if you don't feel particularly thankful. If God gives a command, He expects obedience, whether you are in the mood or not. Thankfulness, like forgiveness, is not an emotion. Thankfulness is an intelligent response of gratitude to God, based on His Word. It is your determination to be obedient.

Here's what to do then: name your sin, and give thanks to God that you *already* are victorious over it. When Jesus died on the cross, He provided forgiveness and freedom. Thank Him for both, saying something like: "Father, I thank You that I am in Christ. I thank You that my position is secure and immovable. Thank You that *in Him* I've already won the victory over the sin which besets me. Thank You that I am free." Soon your experience will catch up with what God has already given you in Christ.

I'm not talking about a once-for-all act of thanksgiving. David wrote, "I will bless the Lord at all times; His praise shall *continually* be in my mouth" (Ps. 34:1, italics added). But how does praise become *a way of life,* a daily habit, more important than tying your shoes or combing your hair?

You don't learn to praise in a day, especially since you may have been complaining for years! New habits take time to develop. But you can begin today, and practice tomorrow, and the next day, until it becomes part of you. "Let the Word of

Christ richly dwell within you, with all wisdom teaching and admonishing one another with psalms and hymns and spiritual songs, singing with thankfulness in your hearts to God'' (Col. 3:16).

Suggested Application

1. Paul lists nine fruits of the Spirit (Gal. 5:22–23). Which two are the most evident in your life? Which two are the least evident?

2. Think specifically of ways in which the fruit of the Spirit can be further developed. These questions might help:

a. What obstacles in your life hinder the ministry of the Spirit? unconfessed sin? strained personal relationships? lack of commitment? little or no time spent in Bible reading or prayer?

b. Have you ever asked God to control you with His Spirit? Remember, we often have not because we ask not (James 4:2). Why not simply thank Him for His control each day, knowing that He will give you strength?

3. The most important ingredient in releasing the Spirit's power in our lives is faith. Our faith is strengthened by (a) making the Word of God the focus of our attention, and (b) developing the habit of praise. Think of creative ways to make these practices a part of your daily activity.

7

THE RENEWING OF
YOUR MIND

You give your anxiety to God, but an hour later its weight is back on your shoulders. You ask God to control your temper, but you blow your top. You pray that you will not lust; you even "reckon" yourself to be dead to sinful impulses. But the next day you can't push that tall blonde out of your mind.

You surrender yourself to God. And then so soon, so easily, revert to your old habits. You mean so well; I mean so well. Yet we fare so poorly. Why?

Jesus told a story that illustrates the most important single principle in breaking a sinful habit. A man who had been inhabited by a demon, rejoiced when that sinister spirit was expelled. The wicked spirit then passed through waterless places, seeking rest. Finding none, it decided to return to its original abode. To its satisfaction, the demon saw that its original house was unoccupied, swept, and put in order. It then found "seven other spirits more evil than itself, and they go in and live there, and the last state of that man becomes worse than the first" (Luke 11:26).

Why did this man fail in his quest for freedom? He didn't understand the principle of *replacement*. None of us can overcome evil by simply renouncing it. Rather, we can only do so by substituting the good in its place. Sinful habits cannot be broken without replacing them with righteous ones.

Try this simple experiment. Think of the number eight. Have you visualized it? If so, exercise your willpower and stop thinking of the number eight right *now*.

Were you able to do it? Of course not. At least, I'm still thinking about that number. Can we, by sheer willpower, stop thinking about the number eight? By no means. Trying to push it out of our minds actually causes us to focus our attention on it.

What a picture of us when we try to overcome sin. We may get on our knees and ask God to take the desire away; we then determine not to think those lurid or greedy thoughts, but there they are again. We resist them once more, trying desperately to push them out of our minds. But we are trapped. Try as we might, we just can't get them to budge.

Can we really be free? Yes, we can control those thoughts, but *not* by trying to stop thinking about them! To simply resist evil is to make it grow stronger. *Our determination not to think lustful thoughts only reinforces them in our thought patterns.*

How, then, can we be free? Let's return to our experiment once more and think of the number eight. Although we can't stop thinking about it by sheer resistance, we can push that number out of our minds quite easily. Here's how: Think of the number one thousand. Then divide it by five. Concentrate on this new information and you'll stop thinking of the number eight.

You can handle sinful thought patterns in the same way. Fear, lust, covetousness—all of these can be squeezed out of your mind by turning your thoughts to the Scriptures. *Freedom comes by filling your mind with God's thoughts.*

I know a young man whose wife died of cancer. She suffered intensely during the last weeks of her life. Yet she and her husband were able to accept this tragedy without bitterness or the slightest trace of self-pity. I asked John, "Why were you and your wife able to accept this so well? Weren't you ever resentful and angry at God through this ordeal?" His reply: "Yes, we had moments like that. But when they came, I read the Scriptures to my wife. Then we bought the whole New Testament on records and we played it in our house, hour after hour." *That* was the secret—expelling angry and anxious thoughts by filling the mind with the Word of God.

What is the best way to take air out of a bottle? Possibly someone could suggest that we build an elaborate vacuum pump to suck out the air. But there is a simpler solution. If you fill the bottle with water, the air has to leave.

To diffuse the power of sin, you need to have your thought patterns replaced by the Word of God. Every temptation, vice, or sinister motive comes to you by your thoughts; these must be brought under the control of the Spirit. Paul wrote, "And do not be conformed to this world, but be transformed by the renewing of your mind, that you may prove what the will of God is, that which is good and acceptable and perfect" (Rom. 12:2). The difference between worldliness and godliness is a renewed mind. The adage puts it succinctly: You aren't what you think you are; but what you think, you are!

Let us suppose you could flash all the thoughts you had last week on a giant screen. Within minutes you would know how you are doing spiritually. Your thoughts not only shape your life; they *are* your life.

A man recently released from prison was having difficulty adjusting to his freedom. He tried this experiment: he took a glass bottle with a distinct shape and crammed it full of wires, some small and some large. After some time had past he smashed the bottle with a hammer. The result? Most of the wires retained the shape of the bottle. Those wires had to be straightened out, one by one.

The man had established his point: it is possible to be technically free and still retain the traits of bondage. Even though a man is liberated, he must adjust to his freedom and carefully dismantle the habits of the past.

As a believer, you are legally free in Christ, but you can still be enslaved by the fantasies of the flesh and the vices of the world. You can yield, surrender, and "pray through," but your mind will revert to familiar territory as soon as your experience wears thin. To leave this self-defeating cycle, you need to outline specific strategy for experiencing the freedom you have in Christ, and accept the victory that is legally yours.

Prepare for Battle

Is this really possible? Yes. But not without locking horns with wicked spiritual forces. Read carefully Paul's words. "For though we walk in the flesh, we do not war according to the flesh, for the weapons of our warfare are not of the flesh, but divinely powerful for the destruction of fortresses. We are destroying speculations and every lofty thing raised up against the knowledge of God, and *we are taking every thought captive to the obedience of Christ*" (2 Cor. 10:3–5; italics added).

You have the spiritual artillery needed to destroy the fortresses of the mind. Vain reasonings, powerful imaginations, and perverted attitudes can be routed. You have the spiritual equipment to track down every thought and make it captive to Christ.

Military moves are made according to determined strategy. Weapons need to be understood before they are used. In this battle with Satan and evil, you need to know the strategy, and be well acquainted with your weapons. Specifically, how can you do this?

1. Identify the alien thoughts that you want replaced. You must name the fantasies, imaginations, and attitudes that you want to get rid of. To say, "I want to be a better Christian," or, "I want to be more joyful," will not do. Generalities are not good. Specifics are needed.

I assume that you know the sins in your life that won't budge. If you have never done it before, now is the time to identify them. Take a sheet of paper and jot down the thought patterns that have to go.

2. *Be prepared for the discipline of spiritual warfare.* The world, the flesh, and the devil do not surrender without a struggle. The person who is blessed by God is one whose "delight is in the Law of the Lord, and in His Law he doth meditate day and night" (Ps. 1:2).

Sometimes we are told, "We are in a spiritual battle. As soldiers of the cross we must be disciplined; we must put effort and sacrifice into the Christian life." Then perhaps a week later, another Christian appears to say the opposite. "I was working too hard at being a Christian; God showed me that I must just hang loose—rest in the Lord."

Though these viewpoints appear contradictory, they really are not. *Only a Christian who is disciplined in the Word of God can rest in the Lord.* Yes, we can cease our striving and learn to relax in the confidence that God is equal to every situation. But a lazy, undisciplined Christian cannot do this; he falls apart at the seams when tragedy strikes. The believer who is like a tree planted by the rivers of water is the one who meditates in the Law of God every free moment; his thoughts turn to the Word of God like steel to a magnet.

Declaring war on your thought life means that you must set aside time every morning to begin your offensive attack. I suggest 20 minutes as a minimum. Meditation in the Scriptures requires effort; nothing worth having can be achieved without exertion.

You've heard the cliché "a chapter a day keeps the devil

away." Don't you believe it. You can read a chapter with your mind on tomorrow's business deal or with a heart full of revenge. Real meditation requires quality time. We must assimilate a passage and give it our unhurried attention.

3. *Be prepared to memorize the Word of God.* "Thy Word I have treasured in my heart, that I may not sin against Thee" (Ps. 119:11). Rather than memorize verses at random, take your list of troublesome thought patterns and find verses of Scripture that speak directly to them. Specific examples are given at the end of this chapter. Memorize these verses so that you have them at your fingertips during the day—you'll need them. The only alternative to memorizing verses is to type them out on small notecards so that you can have them for immediate reference. These are the passages that God will use to demolish the present strongholds of your mind and construct a new edifice.

Use Your Artillery

So far you have your sins identified, you've decided to set aside 20 minutes for God each morning, and you've even got some passages of Scripture to work with. Now what? What should you *do* tomorrow morning? Your strategy begins the moment you awake in the morning. Those moments between waking up and getting your feet on the floor are crucial. The seeds of discouragement, anger, and lust begin here. While still in bed, thank God for the rest He has given to you. Then give the new day to the Lord. Consciously commit your mind, opportunities, and time to Him. Remind yourself of God's promises. Here are a few: "For nothing will be impossible with God" (Luke 1:37). "And we know that God causes all things to work together for good to those who love God, to those who are called according to His purpose" (Rom. 8:28). "I can do all things through Him who strengthens me" (Phil. 4:13). Reminding ourselves of God's promises gives us the proper perspective on life.

Then after you're out of bed and reasonably awake—I need coffee and breakfast to get my mind in gear—read a chapter from the Bible, observing what God is saying to you. Then spend some time to prepare your mind for the particular temptation you will face that day. Let's suppose your boss habitually irritates you. An hour after you arrive at work, you wish you could scream. If you wait until your boss shouts at you before you decide how you will respond, you'll probably react in anger. Use the Word of God in anticipation. During your time with God in the morning, recite the verses you have memorized and claim Christ's victory *before* your boss blows his fuse.

The same principle applies whether your problem is gluttony, addiction, worry, or greed. Claim God's promises for that particular day. Tell Him that with His help you resolve to choose for Him, rather than the world.

But remember, if you wait until temptation comes to decide how you will react, you've waited too long! *Choose beforehand* to claim God's promises for whatever circumstances you expect to encounter.

Then, during the day, learn to obey the first promptings of the Holy Spirit. If you are tempted to enjoy a sensual fantasy, deal with those thoughts *immediately*. Each of us knows when we let our minds skip across that invisible line into forbidden territory. The moment we do so, we sense we are violating the purity that the Holy Spirit desires. That is the moment to say, "I reject these thoughts in the name of Jesus." And then quote the passages of Scripture you have learned for that temptation. With time, your sensitivity to the Holy Spirit will develop.

Most important, learn to switch topics on the flesh and the devil. Remember the experiment at the beginning of this chapter? We couldn't stop thinking of the number eight, no matter how hard we tried. Only switching to another topic could accomplish this result.

You can do this with any temptation you face. Simply use your temptation as an alarm system—a signal to give praise to God. If, for example, you fear cancer (since one out of four people in the U.S. will have the disease, your fears may have a statistical basis), use that fear as an opportunity to give glory to God. Quote Romans 8:35–39 or read Psalms 103, 144, or 145. Then thank God for all the blessings you have in Christ. Thank Him for forgiveness, for His sovereignty, power, and love. In this way, your stumbling block will be changed into a stepping-stone. You'll be praising rather than pouting.

While I've been writing this chapter, a woman called on the phone to ask me to pray that she would overcome her battle with smoking. She's tried to be free, but hasn't succeeded. I gave her several suggestions; one was to accept the desire for a cigarette as a reminder that it is time to read three chapters of praise to God. Rather than concentrating on the desire, she can focus on God and His power. Eventually, she will learn that she does not have to yield to this temptation; the very struggle will become God's way of building discipline into her life.

If your problem is gluttony, decide that your hunger pangs will be a reminder to divert your attention to God's Word. Memorize a verse of Scripture, pray for your missionary friends, sing a song. By outlining and following a specific strategy to resist temptation, you will eventually be free from its grip.

Finally, do not be discouraged by the frequency of the same temptation. If you have lived a long time with sinful thought patterns, the strongholds of your imagination will not be easily toppled. Furthermore, you must recognize the possibility that you are not merely confronting yourself, but satanic forces as well. Satan's most used weapon is discouragement. After you have rejected insidious thoughts, he delights in having them pop back into your mind. Since his activity has become so overt in our society, a later chapter will give specific instruction on how to confront these forces. Let me say in advance that the most important insulation you have against satanic attack is personal righteousness—confessing and forsaking sin. And as you apply the above principles consistently, Satan and his forces will be weakened. Eventually they will flee.

How long does it take for your minds to be renewed? That depends. Some Christians who apply these principles recognize a noticeable difference within a week. Others who are steeped in decades of sin, may need as long as 30 days before they can say, "I am free!" And, of course, no one reaches perfection. The more we meditate on the Word, the more clearly we see new areas of our lives that need to be changed. Subtle motives often surface only after long exposure to the light of God's Word.

A homosexual who was freed from his former way of life by using the above suggestions confessed that he often used to lapse back into his former thought patterns. "But now," he says, "when I think the thoughts I used to think, I get sick to my stomach." He is proof of what God can do in the life of anyone who persistently meditates in the Word of God and applies it directly to areas of spiritual conflict.

I'm convinced that God intends us to be free from mental bondage. His Word is the resource by which our thoughts can become obedient to God.

Even Christ, the eternal Son of God, "learned obedience from the things which He suffered" (Heb. 5:8). "And if He, the Son, sets you free, you shall be free indeed" (John 8:36).

Suggested Application

The following Scripture references can be used to begin the process of bringing your thoughts under the control of the Holy Spirit. Additional passages can be found through careful reading of the Scriptures along with the use of a concordance or *Nave's Topical Bible*.

Covetousness
Psalm 119:36; Luke 12:15; Colossians 3:1–2, 5–6; Philippians 4:11–12; 1 Timothy 6:6; Hebrews 13:5

Pride
Galatians 6:3, 14; James 4:6; 1 Peter 5:5–6

Lack of discipline
Romans 12:11; 1 Corinthians 9:26–27; Philippians 4:12–13; Hebrews 6:12

Lust
Romans 6:11–12; 2 Corinthians 10:4–5; Ephesians 4:22–24; Philippians 4:8; 1 Peter 2:11

Anger
Psalm 37:8; Proverbs 14:29; 16:32; Ephesians 4:26, 31; Colossians 3:8; James 1:19–20

Worry
Matthew 6:25–34; Philippians 4:6; 1 Peter 5:7

Bitterness
Ephesians 4:31–32; Hebrews 12:15

Gluttony
Judges 3:14–22; Proverbs 23:20–21; 1 Corinthians 9:27; 1 Corinthians 10:31–33; Philippians 4:12

8

LIVING WITH
YOUR FEELINGS

Our generation places a high priority on "feeling good." If you watch the ads on TV, you know how this goal is to be reached. First you should be surrounded by the right things—the latest styles in clothing, a new car, a home in the right neighborhood. Second, you should be free of all physical discomfort. If you have a headache, you take a pain killer. In depression, there are stimulants. For tension, depressants. A bumper sticker capsulizes the mood of our culture: "If it feels good, do it!"

It is significant that the first sin ever committed was that of choosing to follow feelings rather than to obey God's commands. The tree would satisfy Eve's hunger; Satan promised her wisdom. She craved and she ate. But her desire was at odds with God's command. Since that time, people have lived according to the dictates of their feelings, indulging the desires of the flesh and mind.

Of course, feelings in themselves are not evil. God created you with the ability to feel pain and joy; Christ Himself is touched with the feeling of your infirmities. To stoically ignore your feelings or reject them out of hand is to invite callousness and indifference. Paul condemned the wicked who were no longer capable of compassion, but were past feeling (Eph. 4:19). But your feelings are not a fully reliable guide for behavior. The feeling of hunger is given by God to keep you alive; without it you would starve. But your craving for food must be kept in check, or else you will probably become gluttonous. Feelings of hunger must be restrained for the total good of the body.

The same can be said for sexual feeling and even feelings of anger and love. Your will must provide a check on the stream of emotions that ebb and flow through your being. If you follow your feelings wherever they may lead, you will be fulfilling virtually every wanton desire.

When I use the word *feeling* I am talking about inclinations, passing preferences, momentary urges. I do not mean those deep currents of emotion which are part of the unity of your person. This book is not to be considered an easy cure for deep emotional disturbances.

I do believe, however, that by self-understanding, by self-control, and by bringing all your feelings—both the surface and the deepest ones—into obedience to Christ and to His Word, that many emotional tragedies can be avoided.

No one part of your being is enough to be your guide. You do not live by thought alone, or by will power, spiritual perception, physical activity, or by feelings, alone. You are a whole person, made in God's image, and no one of these is enough to guide you. Not even all of them together are sufficient.

When Jesus spoke to His tempter, He said, "Man shall not live on bread alone, but on every word that proceeds out of the mouth of God" (Matt. 4:4). He was suggesting the principle of balance, of a life under the authority of the revealed Word of God.

Pitfalls of Living by Feeling

Before I suggest how you can cope with your emotions, I want you to look at what happens when you live by the dictates of your own hunches and whims. A *life based on feelings is an invitation to the sin of disobedience.* Often your feelings run counter to what God requires. In fact, most sinful habits are developed by simply following the path of least resistance, by doing whatever you feel like doing. Many of your struggles can be traced to sensuality, or being controlled by your physical senses. Spiritually, this spawns defeat, negativism, and unbelief.

Many people who think they cannot obey God's commandments really don't feel like obeying. Occasionally they have days when they wake up wanting to do what God requires—but not often. Our fallen human nature seldom feels like obedience; usually it wants to do its own thing. This attitude comes from Satan as he suggests to us—as he did to Eve—that God has asked us to obey commands which we cannot or need not keep. If we think we must *feel* like it, before we obey God's Word, we will never get off the ground in our spiritual lives.

Let's be specific. Suppose love has drained from a marriage. Jay Adams talks about a counseling situation where the partners have already agreed that they will divorce. Neither one has committed a serious sin against the marriage. They just don't feel in love any more. They go to the counselor hoping that he will confirm their decision that if there is no feeling left, the only recourse is divorce. The couple is shocked to find the counselor saying, "If you don't love each other, there is only one thing to do: you will have to *learn* how to love one another." The couple is incredulous. "How can you *learn* to love someone? You can't produce feelings out of thin air!"

The counselor explains that in the Bible God commands us to love one another. When the husband is told that he is to love his wife as Christ loved the church, he gasps. He could never do that.

But the counselor is persistent. He explains that the husband will begin on a lesser level. The Bible also commands us to love our neighbor, and since his wife is his closest neighbor, he is to love her. But even so, the husband objects that he couldn't love his wife that way. Then the counselor explains that the man is still not off the hook, for God has commanded us to love even our enemies! (Jay E. Adams, *You Can Sweeten a Sour Marriage*. Grand Rapids: Baker Book House, 1975)

This couple has made a common error; they are equating love with feelings. In the Bible, love is not a feeling. You can *learn* to love, even though you begin with little or no emotional impetus. In other words, you can *choose* to love. And God gives you the grace to do so.

Love is not an emotion; neither is forgiveness. The Bible commands us to put bitterness away; we are to forgive others whether they solicit our forgiveness or not. Yet many Christians believe that they can't forgive until they *feel* like it! They think that if they forgive when they don't feel like it, they are hypocritical.

However, if forgiveness were an emotion, God would be commanding you to do the impossible. You know that you cannot switch your emotions on and off. You cannot develop the right feelings on your own. But God is not mocking you when He tells you to forgive; you *can* choose to do so, whether you feel like it or not. Never try to skirt God's commands under the pretense that you don't feel like obeying Him.

A second danger of living by feelings is that you may tend to derive your doctrine from feelings. If you believe God is with you just because "He *feels* so close," you will also believe there are days when He forsakes you, because He feels so far away. The assurance of God's presence does not come by feelings, but by faith (Heb. 13:5). Fortunately, you don't always have to feel God's presence to be in fellowship with Him and to make spiritual progress.

The Apostle Paul, who by any standard lived a successful, victorious Christian life, had his bad days. "For we do not want you to be unaware, brethren, of our affliction which came to us in Asia, that we were burdened excessively, beyond our strength, so that we despaired even of life'' (2 Cor. 1:8). Have you ever been restless, not able to control your fluctuating emotions? Paul wrote that he had no rest in his spirit until Titus came to him with some good news from the church (2 Cor. 2:13).

Even more surprising is the testimony of Christ. As He approached the cross, He was tempted to call a halt to the whole plan of redemption. He was deeply vexed in spirit. ''Now My soul has become troubled; and what shall I say, 'Father, save Me from this hour'? But for this purpose I came to this hour. Father, glorify Thy name'' (John 12:27–28a).

His agony in Gethsemane is well documented, as His soul was troubled to the point of death (Matt. 26:38). Emotionally, He shrank from the torture which lay ahead and asked if it were possible that the cup of suffering might pass from Him. All these emotional upheavals took place in the God-Man, the One who lived perfectly, sinlessly.

Now it is true that most depression is the result of sin. It may be your own sin, or the sin of another person against you, and can be most severe if you have concealed the real cause of it—even from yourself. Depression usually originates in self-pity or bitterness or guilt.

A woman who had seen half a dozen counselors could not cope with the intense periods of depression she faced. Despite hours of counsel, she had withheld one important bit of information, namely that as a teenage girl, she had given birth to a baby and had killed it to avoid the stigma attached to her illicit sexual affair. But when she finally admitted her sin and confessed it, and accepted God's forgiveness, the depression left. Self-pity, hostility, and warped values can have the same effect. That is why those who think they have emotional problems often discover that their problems are not really emotional. Indeed, their emotions are working only too well. Their emotional struggles are often symptomatic of unresolved guilt from sin which they have been unwilling to face. Only when the axe is put to the tree does the fruit of sin wither.

However, there are times when you may experience emotional turbulence which may not be related to any particular sin. The cause may be physiological, or perhaps Satan is trying to disrupt your fellowship with God. At any rate, this point needs emphasis: *You do not need to experience a steady stream of placid emotional feelings to walk with God.*

Emotions fluctuate. They are perhaps only little more dependable than the weather. Today you feel great, tonight you can't sleep, and tomorrow life seems pointless. Those moments provide a crucial test of whether you have learned to walk by faith or if you are still dependent on emotional sight. Personally, I'm glad that my acceptance before God is unrelated to the way I feel!

A third consequence of living by feelings is that you develop the sin of procrastination. It's time to visit a friend in the hospital, write a letter, or do some chores at home. You know what you ought to do, but for some mysterious reason you can't seem to get started. You stall, putter around, watch TV; in short, you procrastinate. Why?

There may be several reasons for this. You may feel frustrated because the work seems overwhelming; or you may feel inferior, unable to do the job as well as someone else. So you sit around, waiting for the magic moment when suddenly everything will fall into place. But those magic moments never come, and your responsibilities never go away. The result—you begin to feel guilty for not doing what you ought. Putting matters off does not relieve tension, but increases it.

Perhaps the most tragic consequence of living according to feelings is that such a life ends up being self-defeating. It seems reasonable to believe that the sure path to happiness is to be able to do whatever you feel like doing. But such a person eventually doesn't enjoy his feelings. Shrugging off responsibility only increases guilt. *The more you give in to your feelings, the worse you feel*. Rather than satisfying your feelings, you actually irritate them!

A woman may be depressed because she is unable to finish her housework. She hopes that someday she will feel like ironing clothes, vacuuming the carpet, and carrying out the pile of magazines from the living room. But she doesn't *feel* like it; furthermore, even if she began today, there will be more work tomorrow. She follows her feelings and lies on the sofa, watching TV. Since she is doing what she feels like doing, she should be happy and satisfied, right?

Wrong! Guilt settles upon her like the London fog. Each day she is more behind. The amount of work piles up. Her children and her husband are beginning to complain. But she is so far behind, there is no use trying to catch up. Her frustration will never leave until she chooses to do what she ought, whether she feels like it or not.

The moment you declare war on your besetting sin, you will bump into your feelings, mostly negative ones. Be prepared for a feeling of *helplessness*, an idea that you are the victim of circumstances and desires that you cannot change. This feeling just happens to be the sin of unbelief in a different form. It's one way Satan uses to get us to believe that either God cannot or will not help us.

Very soon, *discouragement* will pry its way into your life. It usually hits a few days after we've decided to make a clean break with sin and develop habits of righteousness. Satan's line goes something like this: "You've tried to break this habit and failed. There is no reason to try again. You're not good enough to expect God to help you."

Another feeling you may have to battle is *laziness*—the notion that you need not put too much effort into the Christian life. You'll want to procrastinate, to put off any serious attempt at seeking God's will concerning your problem. Satan never fears your good intentions. Only your obedience drives him to distraction.

Now take a hard look at your feelings and then ask yourself, "How can I cope with them?"

The Example of Christ in Coping with Your Feelings

Jesus Christ, as fully Man, fully God, experienced all human emotions. He wept at the grave of Lazarus. As He faced the incredible assignment of bearing the sin of the world, He was traumatized by an excruciating emotional burden. Yet Jesus did not spend those last hours in self-pity, bemoaning His fate. He handled the experience constructively, and therefore provides a model for us all. What did He do?

1. Christ admitted His feelings: "My soul is deeply grieved, to the point of death; remain here and keep watch with Me" (Matt. 26:38). He allowed His disciples to have a glimpse at the unutterable passions that came upon Him that dark, oppressive night. To suppress feelings will not cause them to disappear. Feelings must be dealt with honestly, they cannot be ignored. Needless to say, Christ's emotional upheavals did not lead Him to sinful thoughts or behavior, but even so we must follow Him in honestly acknowledging how we feel. Admitting our bitterness, depression, hatred, or passion is the first step in learning to cope with our feelings.

We've all met people who will not admit to their feelings. A pastor told me of one of his deacons who, with a clenched fist and a flushed face, pounded on the table and, with fire in his eyes, shouted, "I'm not angry!"

A woman who recited in meticulous detail all of the wrongs

her husband had committed against her ended her indictment with the startling statement, "Of course I'm not bitter; I've forgiven him for this!" But her careful cataloging of all the wrongs he had done betrayed her. How often we are unwilling to admit how we feel.

David, the psalmist, was vulnerably honest. Read the Psalms, and you will be struck by the wide range of emotions that he felt. When he was joyful, he shouted praises; when he was depressed, he complained about God's silence and apparent indifference to his need. Depression, joy, and even anger were admitted. We don't know how often he told others about his woes, but we know he spent much time giving his problems to God. The first step, then, is to admit the truth about your emotions and tell God how you feel.

2. Christ requested the support of friends. He had three groups of disciples: the 70 who went from house to house to proclaim the kingdom, the 12 who were constantly with Him, and then three within that circle were given special opportunities. Peter, James, and John who had been invited to the Mount of Transfiguration were now asked to help their Master bear His intense suffering. Christ did not consider it beneath His dignity to ask His friends for prayerful intercession and companionship in the hour of trial.

Personally, I believe that many so-called emotional problems could be solved by corporate intercessory prayer. But the church today is much like the disciples who found praying more difficult than sleeping. Their spirit was willing, but the flesh was weak.

3. Christ knew that His emotional suffering would not separate Him from the Father's love and approval. Their relationship was not affected by the weight of His anguish. As believers we need to realize that our acceptance before God is unrelated to our feelings. We do not live the Christian life by moods, but by faith. Freedom comes to us when we understand that our walk with God is not dependent on how we feel when we get out of bed in the morning.

4. Finally, Christ knew that blessing would follow obedience. Emotional peace and calm would come *after* doing God's will and not before. The assurance of joy in the future enabled Him to endure the tortures of the present. As you pursue victory over the "sin which so easily entangles," you can fix your "eyes on Jesus who for the joy set before Him endured the cross, despising the shame, and has sat down at the right hand of the throne of God" (Heb. 12:2).

Remember that *feelings flow from action and not vice versa.* You can prove this tomorrow morning. If you follow your feelings, you will not get out of bed when the alarm clock rings. To wait for the proper feeling will mean that your day will begin behind schedule. But if you choose to get up and take a shower, whether you feel like it or not, you will soon discover that you are feeling pretty good. And by the time you have finished your breakfast, you will be thinking that life isn't so bad after all. Proper feelings come because of action; they do not precede the action itself.

Whenever we obey God, our feelings begin to fall in line; we have a sense of satisfaction, a sense of self-esteem. To seek the proper feelings first will inevitably lead to despair. Yet there are still some Christians waiting for that magic moment when they will feel like obeying, feel like committing themselves to God, and feel like praying and reading their Bible!

Every one of us has tasks we dislike doing. What makes us think that we should wait until we feel like doing them? Christ did not feel like dying on the cross. He suffered more physical pain than most of us can comprehend, along with an excruciating moral anguish, as the sinless One became identified with the sin of the world. Every emotional conflict known to man (except personal guilt) convulsed within the body of the Son of God. But

He went ahead with it because He was obedient unto death, even the death of the cross. Why did He do it? Jesus knew that *after obedience there is joy.* How often we have reversed the order. We think we've got to be in the right mood to obey God. But there is no joy until there is obedience.

One final word: *we must learn to give thanks to God for all things, whether we feel like it or not.* The focus of our attention must be the truth that is settled in heaven.

Several years ago, I experienced a period of depression. I learned that depression is real; it's not just a fantasy. The evening it hit, life seemed so useless. The phrase that kept popping into my head was, "Vanity of vanities, all is vanity." I had always told others that the cure for depression was praise. Now it was time to take a shot of my own medicine.

Months before this incident, I had prepared a list of all the blessings that God has given us in Christ. Resisting all my negative emotional impulses, I began to thank God for each one. Even though I didn't *feel* thankful, I was grateful mentally, and I told God so. Even reciting the verses of Scripture and giving thanks seemed to be so futile. Yet I continued, resisting the thought of quitting. It wasn't long before the depression left. Of course, I'm not suggesting that all depression can be handled so simply. But in tackling our emotional moods, praise is the place to begin.

I've discovered a new liberty in my Christian life since I have realized that my faith need not be tied to my feelings. We honor God when we walk by faith without emotional supports. And within time, our feelings begin to catch up with the truth that we accept with our minds. In practical terms, this means that we can begin right *now* to take constructive steps toward positive change. We'll never feel more like doing it than at this very moment. The suggested application at the end of this chapter will help you to begin right *now.*

Suggested Application

1. What evidence is there that our generation stresses physical comfort (feelings and pleasure) rather than a life of self-denial?

2. "Faith often runs counter to feeling. Even the attempt to find victory in feelings is a sin in the life of a believer. In short, it is simply 'walking in the flesh.' We must repent of the sin of assessing the reality of the Christ-life on the basis of feeling."— Henry Teichrob Discuss or think over this statement with questions such as these in mind: Why do our feelings fluctuate? Why do we so often think that spirituality is to be equated with "feeling just right"? Give examples where faith runs contrary to feelings.

3. What responsibilities do you have which you do not *feel* like doing? Why do you then do them? What would happen if you only did whatever you felt like doing?

4. Read the words of Christ in John 12:27–28. How does the text show that Christ's determination to do the Father's will often went counter to His own feelings?

5. What practical benefits are there in realizing that we walk by faith and not emotional sight?

9

THE TAMING OF YOUR WILL

You have heard someone who is on a diet say, "I just don't have any willpower!" How frustrating to know what you ought to do and yet not do it! The gap between knowledge and performance is often embarrassing. You just can't seem to get yourself moving in the right direction. Yet, unless you can use your will effectively, you will be paralyzed in your Christian life.

Can your will be disciplined? Yes. You do not need to drift aimlessly through life, carried like a cork on a river. You can learn to make responsible decisions and say No to the path of least resistance.

What Is Your Will?

Your will is your decision-making faculty. Often it is caught between your thoughts and your desires. Your emotions express how you feel; your mind says what you know, but your will tells what you *want*. The weary disciples experienced this tension in Gethsemane. Christ asked them twice to watch with Him, but they fell asleep. Our Saviour commented, "Keep watching and praying that you may not enter into temptation; the spirit is willing, but the flesh is weak" (Matt. 26:41).

Let's move this problem closer to home—to your own bedroom, for instance. The alarm rings at 6:00 A.M. and your mind knows full well what that means: you should carefully move from a horizontal to a vertical position. But your body feels differently about the matter. Now your will has to make a decision which cannot satisfy both the body and the mind. And your will has only a few moments to decide or you will drift into unconscious comfort for another hour.

What determines whether your will follows the direction of the mind or the inclinations of the body? It depends on your desires and your determination to fulfill these desires. If your job is important to you, you'll be strongly inclined to get out of bed. If your temporary comfort is more attractive than a paycheck, you'll tend to ignore the alarm clock.

If you were born into a home with little discipline and weak commitment to dependability, you'll have a strong tendency to do whatever comes naturally. However, background cannot be used as an excuse for laziness, because those who were reared in well-disciplined homes fight the same natural desires. Believe it or not, we are all much the same *inside!*

Thank God that you need not be controlled by your environment. The power of the Gospel can set you free from the conditioning of your home or society. You can choose, by God's grace, to change, to refuse to be pressed into the mold of your past.

Heredity also influences the will. We've all inherited from the temperaments of our parents. Those who have studied human nature believe they have discovered several distinct behavioral patterns. Every one of us is a combination of these temperaments.

But more important than your heredity or environment is the fact that you were born with a sinful nature, a natural tendency to do evil rather than good. *By nature,* you indulge the desires of the flesh and of the mind. Your will is paralyzed, unable to choose the righteousness which God requires. Left to yourself, you would never choose God.

If you are unconvinced, read Romans 3:10–11: "There is none righteous, not even one; there is none who understands, there is none who seeks for God." By yourself you aren't even able to seek God.

Twentieth-century man has a great obsession with freedom. But his freedom, if it exists, is severely limited. At best, modern man is able to pursue his own passions, fulfill his own lusts, and choose his own goals. He is not free to seek after God. How, then, can he be saved?

Christ taught that no man can come to Him unless the Father draws him (John 6:44–65). God does not save you by circumventing your will. He works through it, giving you the ability to choose. You have heard the expression, "Let go and let God," implying that God will take over and control you completely if you wish Him to do so. But this is not biblical. Your will does not become passive when you yield to God. A surrendered will experiences struggle, as Christ's conflict in Gethsemane demonstrates.

Fortunately, the Holy Spirit does not stop working with man's will at the time of conversion. Paul wrote, "And for this purpose also I labor, striving according to His power, which mightily works within me" (Col. 1:29). The Comforter stands ready to come to your aid the moment you face a temptation or have a decision to make.

The Basis of Choice

Before you can bring your will into harmony with God's purposes, you need adequate goals for your life. If you don't believe that life is worth living, it won't make much difference to you if you break sinful habits or reinforce them. A purposeful life, therefore, is the basis for discipline and determination to make right choices.

Day-to-day activities have short-term meaning. If you choose to clean the house, mow the lawn, or write a chapter of a book, you have a sense of satisfaction when the task is completed. Specific short-term goals give direction in how you use your time.

But temporary goals are not adequate for a meaningful and satisfying life. An insurance executive who had achieved all the short-term goals you can imagine—two beautiful homes, cars, and plenty of vacation time—committed suicide recently because "life wasn't worth the trouble of living." He had reached all of his materialistic goals and found they were not ultimately satisfying. *Only eternal values can give meaning to temporal ones.* Time must be the servant of eternity. Let's look at how this can be applied.

1. The example of Moses. Moses could say No to the world because he was firmly convinced that time (or eternity, if you please) would vindicate his choice. Focusing on the eternal gave him the resources to make wise choices on earth.

Given his values, Moses was willing to forego immediate pleasures. The Bible does not deny there is pleasure in short-term goals. In Pharaoh's court, Moses could have enjoyed wine, women, and song, and far-flung political power as well. But he knew that such pleasures are short-lived. He was able to postpone his immediate desires because of his faith in future rewards. He could say No to the world without thinking he had been shortchanged.

In the record of the faithful ones, Hebrews 11, we read, "By faith Moses, when he had grown up, refused to be called the son of Pharaoh's daughter; choosing rather to endure ill-treatment with the people of God, than to enjoy the passing pleasures of sin; considering the reproach of Christ greater riches than the treasures of Egypt; for he was looking to the reward. By faith he left Egypt, not fearing the wrath of the king; for he endured, as seeing Him who is unseen" (Heb. 11:24–27).

Moses endured, because he saw the invisible One. He saw the difference between time and eternity. Paul wanted the Corinthian Christians: to "look not at the things which are seen, but at the things which are not seen; for the things which are seen are temporal, but the things which are not seen are eternal" (2 Cor. 4:18).

Contrast this with the immaturity of the "now" generation, wanting all of its kicks, thrills, and highs at this very moment. No consideration is given for tomorrow, much less the distant future. The permanent is sacrificed on the altar of the immediate.

Those who trust God can postpone fulfillment of their desires. Sex can wait until marriage; the discipline of hard study can be endured for the sake of an education; and any sinful pleasure can be abandoned in favor of the greater pleasure of fellowship with God.

2. The example of Christ. Jesus knew where He had come from, why He was here, and what He was supposed to accomplish. He came down from heaven, not to do His own will, but the will of the Father. That determination controlled every decision He made.

As a result, He was not distracted with trivia. He was never in a hurry, for He knew His Father would not give a task without the time to do it. Christ was not driven by crises, feeling He must heal everyone in Israel. He could say, "It is finished," even when many people were still bound by demons and twisted by disease. What mattered ultimately was not the number of people healed or fed, but whether the Father's will was being done. His clearly defined goals simplified His decisions.

We too need such a singleness of purpose. Specific goals will motivate us to do the will of God. Once we know where we are going, it's much easier to get there; indeed, the journey becomes a pleasure. Dr. Ari Kiev, of Cornell Medical Center, states, "Observing the lives of people who have mastered adversity, I have repeatedly noted that they have established goals and, irrespective of obstacles, have sought with all their effort to achieve them. From the moment they've fixed an objective in their minds and decided to concentrate all their energies on a specific goal, they begin to surmount the most difficult odds" (Ari Kiev, *A Strategy for Daily Living*. New York: Free Press, 1973, p. 3).

How Do We Set Goals?

The invisible is more valuable than the visible. The eternal is more enduring than the temporal. But what do these facts have to do with your values, your goals?

Your goals are set on the foundation of your larger beliefs about life and about yourself. Within the framework of your ultimate commitments you formulate your short-range goals.

Let me suggest three levels of commitment that are appropriate for the Christian: (1) commitment to God in Christ, (2) commitment to the body of Christ, and (3) commitment to the *work* God has given you to do. These three levels are the outline in which you can specify what you want to accomplish with your life. It is your responsibility to creatively spell out how you plan to fulfill these commitments. For example, your commitment to God might mean that you spend a half an hour each day getting to know the One to whom you have committed yourself. You may want to cut the time you spend watching TV. Of course, you'll want to specify your plans to study the Bible, what book you'll begin with, etc.

You will want to set goals in other parts of your life too. You may want to lose 30 pounds or even 15. A body redeemed by God should not be victimized by gluttony. Once you decide how much weight you plan to lose and the diet you will follow—stay with it! Choose to forego immediate desires. When you are tempted by foods that are not on your diet, remind yourself that this immediate pleasure can be postponed. Your goal to reduce means more to you than the craving for excess food. Remember that the benefits of proper body size far outweigh obesity! So say No to your desires.

Of course, the value of such discipline will reach into such everyday activities as getting out of bed in the morning, carrying out the garbage, or washing windows. You can bring your body under control and do what you ought, what is in line with the goals you set. If you value your commitments enough, then saying that No or Yes will be doing what you really want—long term.

Your momentary feelings are not a good guide toward fulfilling desirable goals. Paul had his body in control: "But I buffet my body and make it my slave, lest possibly, after I have preached to others, I myself should be disqualified" (1 Cor. 9:27). There is simply no way to give in to all the desires of the body. You'd be dead inside of a week if you did!

Your Will Is Your Want-to

The invisible is more valuable than the visible. It is good to set priorities, to have goals. But what about your *want to?* Your will? How are you going to hold to these goals you are setting that fit into your belief about God's will for your life?

Setting good goals is not easy. And staying with them is harder yet. As a Christian you need and have available the help of God as you seek to do His Will. And yet it is just at this point—of your will and God's will—that there is conflict.

The struggle between your self-will and God's will is intense. You were born with the desire to control your own destiny, to do "your own thing." Consequently, your fallen will is adept at making choices in harmony with your pride, independence, and self-determination. You resist the idea that God should rule over you, particularly when He begins to meddle in your private affairs.

You don't want God to decide whether or not you have a marriage partner. You don't want to submit your plans to a higher authority for approval. If you want to spend your Sunday afternoon watching football, that ought to be *your* decision. Or if you are skimpy in giving your money to the local church, that is *your* business. Entrusting yourself wholly to God seems rather impractical. If you don't take care of yourself, who will? You have to look out for Number One!

It is just this kind of attitude that needs to learn obedience and humility. Usually we think that the human will must be strengthened, but paradoxically *you become stronger only when you become weaker*. When you surrender your will to God, you finally discover the resources to *do* what God requires. As you give yourself to Him, you receive His power.

When you are at the end of your rope, God is there to catch you—but not before. David knew that the most he could offer God was a yielded will, "The sacrifices of God are a broken spirit; a broken and a contrite heart, O God, Thou wilt not despise" (Ps. 51:17).

Submission to God always involves humility; it is an acknowledgment that you are neither qualified nor able to do what you ought to. Your temptation to strive with the Almighty is ever with you.

A businessman woke up early one Saturday morning and went golfing with friends. He knew that there was a men's meeting at the church, part of a revival that was in progress. When he finished playing 18 holes, it was noon. His curiosity made him stop at the church on his way home. He hoped the meeting would be over. But if not, he would at least "check to see who is there." To his amazement, half of the men were on their knees, many of them weeping. Others had left the room for special prayer.

He let all of this register for a moment and then angrily clenched his fist and slammed it into his other hand, and said, "You'll never get me, God!"

Get him for what? What would make a Christian say this? The matter most pressing on his mind was his relationship with his children. The man was victimized by a hot temper, and many times had hurt his children's feelings and wounded their spirits. He knew that if God "got" him, he would have to humble himself and ask the forgiveness of his children. He decided that the price was too great.

When you fight against the demands of God, trying to weasel out of whatever doesn't suit you, your will is pitted against God in a desperate struggle for survival.

But when you say Yes to God, you discover the ability to do His will. Strength is dependent upon surrender.

God did "get" the businessman. He humbled himself and went to his children to ask their forgiveness. Later, as he told how God had broken him, he wept unashamedly. God gave him the willpower to do what he could not do on his own. And his will was energized by the Holy Spirit when he stopped resisting and chose to say No to his sin. At that point it became possible for God to work through the man's will to accomplish His purpose.

You Can Lessen the Conflict

Does temptation ever lose its power? Not completely. Even when we are motivated by a desire to please God, we experience conflict, because God often requires obedience that runs counter to human motivations.

Christ Himself expressed this conflict: "For I have come down from heaven, not to do My own will, but the will of Him who sent Me'' (John 6:38). He voluntarily set aside any personal ambitions and submitted Himself to His Father's will.

The conflict between your immediate interests and God's long range goals is not just going to go away. But there is an answer. For when you begin to commit yourself to God, the Holy Spirit begins to resolve these conflicts. He pulls the fragments of your life together. He shows you His truth as a standard for making choices. He teaches you a single-mindedness that you never knew before. He shows you the rewards of living in His love and justice. And after a while, you begin to realize that in many instances, what God *requires* of you is really what you *want* to do.

This helps us understand Christ's conflict. True, His human inclinations ran contrary to what the Father's will required. Paul says that Christ did not please Himself (Rom. 15:3). But much greater than the natural desire to avoid suffering was His satisfaction in doing God's will. The prophet predicted that Christ would say, ''I delight to do Thy will, O My God'' (Ps. 40:8).

Visualize a piece of steel suspended between two magnets. It vacillates, unsure of whether it should swing to the right or to the left. For a moment, it wavers. It could go either way, because it is being simultaneously drawn in two directions. Then, as it swings toward the right, it wavers for a second and continues to move in the same direction. Now it moves more rapidly to the right; it cannot swing back any more. It is out of the range of the left magnet's power.

You may be hovering between God and the world. Now it is your desires, now it is God's. No one knows what your eventual decision will be. *But the farther you go in God's direction, the less attraction the world will have*. The day will come when your choices will be easier. Saying Yes to God can be habit-forming.

There is another lesson you can learn from this illustration. *You can't say No to temptation unless you say Yes to God.* Like the magnet, the world will never lose its power to attract. To merely resist its power is pointless; no will is strong enough. But what you do is focus your attention on God as revealed in the Scriptures. Then you remove yourself from the sphere of the world's influence.

I have found that I can't resist enticing thoughts simply by saying, "I resist that thought!" The thought returns again and again. I do, however, have the ability to switch my thoughts to the Scriptures—quote a verse, offer praise, or renew my fellowship with God. Only in the presence of the Almighty does the world lose its lure.

God has given you the resources to say No to sin. Paul urged his readers to obey, but not merely by appealing to their unaided human wills. He reminded them that "it is God who is at work in you, both to will and to work for His good pleasure" (Phil. 2:13). God works in us by energizing our will. He helps us make the decisions that we ought to make, and ultimately really want to make.

God uses your struggles with temptation to teach you how to depend on His power. The ninth fruit of the Spirit is self-control. That word, *self-control,* means literally "to hold oneself in." It refers to the mastery of desires—in the interest of higher ideals.

Don't feel powerless against a barrage of temptations. Maybe you have an insatiable desire for drugs, alcohol, and excess calories. Maybe your sins are restricted to your mind. Whatever your sins, there is hope. Like Christ, Moses, and an innumerable host of saints before you, you can say No to any stubborn habit, by setting the right priorities. And the more you learn to love Christ, the less you will be attracted by the world.

Suggested Application

1. Read Psalm 73, the story of Asaph who began to wonder whether serving God was worthwhile. Notice particularly how his problem was solved when he began to focus on eternal rather than temporal rewards.

2. Ponder Proverbs 25:28. Describe the characteristics of someone who has no control over his spirit. What are the advantages of being disciplined?

3. Take an inventory of your life by asking: In what areas am I resisting God's complete ownership? Suggested areas might be: time, pleasures, recreation, vocation, health, reputation, marital status, friendships, etc. Pray right now and give these areas fully to God.

4. Think of two responsibilities you have which you most *dis*like. Why are they so difficult? Depend on God for strength to do one of those *right now* or sometime today.

5. If you have not already done so, set aside 20 minutes each morning to begin the day with God. You'll be tempted not to follow through with your commitment. List what those temptations might be and develop a strategy to combat them.

10

THE INTERCESSION OF CHRIST AND BELIEVERS

Susan was planning to die on August 22, 1972. She had been a believer for 12 years and had no doubt that she was God's child. She taught Sunday School, witnessed, and tried to live "a good Christian life."

But now she was experiencing prolonged periods of depression. Her health was failing, and pressures in the home had become unbearable. Two of the older children were rebellious. Susan couldn't cope with it all. She had looked to her husband for support and felt that he was insensitive and cold; he just didn't understand what she was going through. She read books to find an answer, but nothing seemed to help. Her only relief was in tranquilizers and sleeping pills. She felt she was alone in the struggle and no one else could help her.

The next step was to contemplate divorce. She recalls, "I wanted out and fast." Her husband had recently committed himself to Christ at a meeting in their home church. Susan was glad; *he* needed it. But now she began to think her husband didn't love her any more. He just walked around with a smile on his face, completely relaxed, and seemed more insensitive than ever.

Susan had had enough of everything, including life itself. She awoke on August 22 and meticulously planned her last day on earth: she would help her sixteen-year-old son get his driving permit and perhaps even straighten out a few things in the house. Her sleeping pills were with her. She was at peace, confident that she had made the right decision.

When she arrived back home with her son, she went to change clothes. "Where are you going?" her son asked. "To the ladies' meeting at the church," she answered thoughtlessly. "Do you have to?" he responded.

Susan did not want to go, but decided that she would. Unusual events had been going on at the church; in fact, a revival was in progress. The ladies were having a special meeting.

Still confident that this would be her last day on earth, she cried the four miles to the church. "Lord," she prayed, "I know John will be better off with a new wife; the children will be better off with a different mother."

Trembling, she entered the sanctuary. The smiles on the women's faces only amplified her own depression. She did not participate in the singing. Instead, she wept for 15 minutes.

When they stopped for lunch, she would not eat. She had been without food for four days and didn't plan to eat now. A woman invited her to come to the prayer room for some counsel. Susan's struggle was intense. She had not planned on confessing her sins and yielding herself to God. But four other women joined her; they read the Scriptures with her and then they began to pray. There on their knees, the women interceded for Susan. An hour passed before the long ordeal was over. When Susan emerged from the prayer room, she recalls that she "had no thought of death. I had never felt so alive in all my life."

Six months later she wrote, "Even though Satan has buffeted me a number of times, I can say that God does all things well, because truly His power is shown in weakness. I do have a health problem—but the depression is gone."

Susan's experience illustrates an important biblical principle: *we cannot successfully live the Christian life on our own.* God never intended that any one of us experience either failure or success alone, independent of the body of Christ. We need God's people for encouragement and intercession, and for the strength that comes from close fellowship.

And perhaps more importantly, we need the intercession of Christ as well. Our sin is never a private matter. We cannot say, "It only hurts me." God, Christ, and Satan are involved in our failures, whether public or private. Satan accuses us before the Father; the Son intercedes; and the Father gives the verdict. Lewis Sperry Chafer used to say, "A secret sin on earth is an open scandal in heaven."

The Intercession of Christ

Whenever tragedy strikes a family, the people who can be of most comfort are those who have had a similar experience. A widow can minister to another widow; bereaved parents are helped by the support of others who have lost a child. There are two reasons for this. First, it's encouraging to know that others have survived a similar difficulty. Then second, all of us want to meet someone who *knows* how we feel.

Christ qualifies on both counts. He experienced every temptation we've ever encountered. He was assaulted by Satan and hounded by physical distress. He faced hunger, rejection, and death successfully. And today, He is deeply moved by our own feelings and struggles. True, He doesn't have a sin nature; but the excruciating pain of the cross, coupled with the horror of being identified with sin, was more torment than we could ever bear. That's why the Scriptures can say, "For we do not have a High Priest who cannot sympathize with our weaknesses, but One who has been tempted in all things as we are, yet without sin" (Heb. 4:15). Today Christ says to us, "I *know* how you feel." Furthermore, He is moved with compassion—sympathy, if you please—for our weaknesses.

Can we confront Satan and win? Can we experience death and arrive safely on the other side? Christ did and *in Him* we can too! Because He endured His temptations, He offers all of us hope. Today He is at the right hand of God the Father, making intercession for us. His presence reminds the Father that we have been bought at high cost. When we sin, He takes up our case and assumes all of the legal aspects of our relationship with God (1 John 2:1).

An example of His power of intercession is seen in the life of Peter. After the Lord's Supper was instituted, Christ said to him, "Simon, Simon, behold Satan has demanded permission to sift you like wheat; but I have prayed for you, that your faith may not fail; and you, when once you have turned again, strengthen your brothers" (Luke 22:31–32).

Peter retorted, "Lord, with You I am ready to go both to prison and to death!" (v. 33) Christ was not impressed; He knew Peter. Moments later, this rugged fisherman would deny Christ and curse as well. His courage would turn to cowardice in a matter of minutes.

Was Christ's prayer answered? Yes! Peter did deny Christ, but the story doesn't end there. It says, "He went outside and wept bitterly" (v. 62). After his repentance, he was able to comfort and strengthen others. His ministry, as recorded in the Book of Acts, and his letters to the young and suffering church, are proof that Christ's prayer was answered.

Satan sifted Peter and discovered that he was part chaff and part wheat. But because of the intercession of Christ, the chaff was blown away and the wheat became nourishment for others in need.

Today God gives Satan permission to do the same to us. Temptation, struggles, and failures are all part of the process.

Most of us, like Peter, are a mixture of chaff and wheat, as our track record shows. But near to uphold us, keep us, and come to our aid is our Lord, who is qualified to keep us from stumbling irrevocably. "For since He Himself was tempted in that which He has suffered, He is able to come to the aid of those who are tempted" (Heb. 2:18).

What an encouragement! Think again about that sin in your life that you can't seem to conquer. The outcome of that struggle is intensely important to God. It's a contest between Christ and Satan, and you happen to be the trophy!

But Christ is not the only one who intercedes for us. He invites all believers to participate in this rewarding ministry. Remember Christ's intercession in Gethsemane? He was struggling with the prospect of the Cross and asked His disciples to *watch with Him*. Three times He asked them to participate in His agony. They failed because they were too weary, but the invitation was there. Christ gives us the same opportunity. We can intercede with Him on behalf of other believers. We're invited to join Him in a ministry of intercession.

The Intercession of Believers

Sometimes our besetting sin won't budge until we enlist the prayer support of God's people, particularly where there is addiction to alcohol, drugs, sexual misconduct, or calories; we need the added support of others who will *stand in for us* in the presence of God. Recently, after I had spoken at a church meeting, a young woman who is a lesbian came up to talk to me. She feels she is morally weak; in fact, she isn't even sure she wants to change her lifestyle. She needs the persistent prayers and encouragement of God's people to help her come to terms with her problem.

Why is this necessary? Why doesn't an all-powerful God just give us victory if we individually apply the right principles? On the surface, it seems odd that my failure or success should be determined by other believers' faithfulness or negligence. Why the need for others to become involved?

Primarily, it is because God wants us to give up our independent spirit. By nature, we are creatures who prefer to live according to our own blueprint. How we live is our business— what right does anyone have to ask or even be interested in how we are progressing spiritually? If we want them to know, we'll tell them!

The New Testament teaches otherwise. We are all members of the body of Christ, and each of us affects the function of others. If you have ever had a toothache, you know that the parts of your body are not isolated. When one tooth aches, your whole body hurts.

Have you ever seen a human hand severed from a body? It looks gruesome. Yet, attached to an arm and connected to the nervous system, the hand is not only highly useful, but beautiful too. The difference lies in its relationship to the body. Similarly, in Christ *no individual is anything if cut off from the body.*

That's why God wants us to enlist the resources of other believers. It's humbling to realize that we need their support and help, but we do. Our struggles and temptations remind us that successes or failures are always a team effort. There's no room in the body of Christ for an individual score card.

That's why we must be acquainted with God's people. It is good to form friendships in church, where committed believers gather for fellowship and instruction. Within the larger circle of believers, we find that there are those who become our special friends. As we develop confidence in them, we can turn to them in the time of need. At that moment, we are tapping a reservoir of spiritual power. "For where two or three have gathered together in My name, there am I in their midst" (Matt. 18:20). The first responsibility of God's people is persistent prayer for one another; not merely individual prayer, but corporate prayer. Prayer *as a group* is important.

Recently, I talked to a couple who was deeply hurt because a child they had adopted was taken away from them by the child's natural mother. Hopelessly neurotic and bitter, she had found her son and kidnapped him. Understandably, this Christian couple, who had accepted this boy from birth, was deeply upset. "Everyone is praying for us, but there's been no break in the case," the distraught woman told me. When I asked if people met with them for prayer, she responded, "No, but they all say they are praying for us." My suggestion to her was that they select a group of people, perhaps six, to meet with them regularly for prayer. It's not enough for people to say, "We're praying." There is supportive value in sharing our heartbreaks with a group of God's people. Christ, you will recall, wanted the disciples to be at His side during His agony in Gethsemane. It wasn't only their prayers that He wanted. He wanted someone to be with Him during those agonizing moments, giving encouragement.

A second way others can help us is by being people to whom we can be responsible and accountable. We can agree to report to the group, or at least to one individual, on our spiritual progress. If I know someone is going to ask me, "How's that problem coming?" I'm going to be more inclined to flee from temptation. One man suggested to his friend, "Whenever you are tempted to take another drink, call me collect, any time of day, and we'll pray together over the phone."

That's a great idea! When I was in seminary, a close friend of mine and I met together for sharing and prayer every Thursday evening at 9:30. We were able to be honest with each other, giving a report on our failures and successes. Knowing about that appointment was an incentive to me. I found that I was watching my actions so that I would not let my friend down. Of course, if we do fail, we need to be honest. Our pride would want us to say that all is well when it is not. But when we develop responsibility toward others, it helps us do what we ought.

This practice of checking on each other can be used in many different ways. A month ago, another friend of mine and I agreed to learn the essential teaching of one chapter of the Bible per day. Occasionally, we call each other on the telephone just to check on how we are doing. "What's in chapter 12?" he'll ask, and I've got to know it cold. When I'm tempted to let the project slide, I remind myself of that commitment and how I'd feel if I were to flunk his quiz.

A homosexual told me that he would not go downtown without the companionship of another Christian. The man simply could not trust himself. The temptation to slide back into his former ways was too strong. But with a Christian companion along, he would not succumb to such enticement. Later, when he became stronger, spiritually, he did not need such support.

God wants to teach us, then, that we cannot live a successful Christian life independent of His children. If we are wayward, we must be restored; if we are weak, others must share their strength with us. At no time ought we to think that we are making it alone with God—for we need His redeemed people, too.

Restoring a Believer

What should we do when we see a fellow believer trapped in a sinful habit? Discuss the matter with our friends? Or do nothing, hoping that someday he will snap out of it?

The Bible is explicit about our responsibility. If our believer has erred, and not merely violated our personal preferences, it is our *duty* to restore him, to help him rectify his relationship with God. Jesus instructed, "And if your brother sins, go and reprove him in private; if he listens to you, you have won your brother. But if he does not listen to you, take one or two more with you, so that by the mouth of two or three witnesses every fact may be confirmed. And if he refuses to listen to them, tell it to the church; and if he refuses to listen even to the church, let him be to you a Gentile and a tax-gatherer" (Matt. 18:15–17).

Our first responsibility is to *go to him in private*. Don't tell your friends, your relatives, or even your pastor! At this point, there is no reason to make the sin public. If the brother is repentant and is given instruction on how to break from that sin, there is no reason for others to become involved.

We've all disobeyed God on this score. Confronting another believer in love takes courage, so we prefer the cowardly route of gossip. We pass the news to others, thinking they should help, or at least "pray." Baser motives often lie beneath such excuses. We delight in other people's faults because it gives us an exalted feeling of superiority. "We'd never do *that*."

Churches have been split and family relationships shattered beyond repair because we have not had the courage to go to a fellow Christian caught in a sin. Matters that should have been cared for in private have mushroomed into bitter confrontations when people have chosen sides on the issues. Such is the price of cowardice. More accurately, such is the fruit of disobedience.

Paul gave some instructions regarding our attitude in the restoration process. If the person's sin is generally known, the church should select qualified men to confront the believer in love. "Brethren, even if a man is caught in any trespass, you who are spiritual restore such an one in a spirit of gentleness; looking to yourselves, lest you too be tempted" (Gal. 6:1). We've already mentioned that sin in another person's life tends to generate self-righteousness in us. We like to feel superior, and to believe that we are immune to such temptation. That type of an attitude will stifle any attempt to restore the believer. Paul warns that we dare not come across as super-Christians We must go in humility, knowing full well that we could slide into the same trespass.

Of course, the initial contact is not the end of it. We must be prepared to befriend, counsel, and pray with those who hurt. God wants every one of us to have a ministry in the life of another believer. I don't mean that this ministry must be one-sided; we'll soon discover that we cannot help others without being edified in return. It's not that part of the body of Christ should be dependent on another part. We *all* need to be dependent on each other. Anything less than this fosters a kind of individualism that is sin.

Suggested Application

1. Read 1 Corinthians 12. What responsibility does one member of the body of Christ have to another? Give specific examples. Why do you think that believers do not help each other as they ought?

2. Try to become a member of a small group of believers who pray together and support one another spiritually. Learn to share your concerns and struggles with them. Think of creative ways that the group could better help one another grow in Christ.

3. In what ways have churches often given the impression that they are not interested in helping those with special needs? What can be done to change this impression—or fact?

4. Christ is our Representative in heaven: what specifically would you want Him to request the Father on your behalf? Now remember that *you* have the same access to the Father because of your position in Christ (John 16:23–27). Use your opportunity to speak to Him directly through Christ.

11

RESISTING SATANIC ACTIVITY

OK. So you're still defeated. You've tried to follow the principles we've covered so far. You've had some successes, but mostly failures. Your passions are so strong, your behavioral ruts so deep. There were moments you were optimistic, but you're back to that habit: eating too many calories, overcome by sexual lust or the victim of negative attitudes. What has gone wrong?

I've learned through the study of the Bible and personal experience that *both* the flesh and satanic forces are involved in our spiritual struggles. I used to believe that the only time we confronted satanic activity was in cases of bizarre behavior or when dabbling in the occult.

But consider the case of Ananias and Sapphira, mentioned in Acts 5. You'll recall they lied about the amount of money they received from the sale of their land. Let's assume they sold their land for $1,000, but when asked how much they got for it, they replied, "Six hundred dollars." In one sense, they spoke the truth—they *had* sold it for $600, though they failed to say it was $600 plus $400! So that is a white lie—what some people call a white one.

Who would guess that Satan was the instigator of this deception? Yet Peter comments, "Ananias, why has Satan filled your heart to lie to the Holy Spirit, and to keep back some of the price of the land?" (Acts 5:3) Be assured that the father of lies is involved when we tell a lie—even a white one.

Does Satan play a role in the breakup of the marriage bond? Paul warns that couples ought to meet one another's sexual needs, "lest Satan tempt you because of your lack of self-control" (1 Cor. 7:5b). Again, Satan is there, doing whatever he can to ruin a marriage.

Let us suppose that your sin is cowardice. You just can't seem to open your mouth for Christ. You feel awkward and embarrassed to be identified with Him. Could these thoughts be instigated by satanic powers? When Peter denied Christ, our Lord remarked that it was Satan who demanded that Peter be sifted as wheat (Luke 22:31). Yes, Satan was actively involved in Peter's denial of Christ. The evil one also hindered Paul from visiting the church at Thessalonica (1 Thes. 2:18); he is the originator of false doctrine, and the deceived are held captive by him to do his will (2 Tim. 2:26). Satan obscures the issues of the Gospel and blinds the minds of the unsaved ". . . that they might not see the light of the Gospel of the glory of Christ, who is the image of God" (2 Cor. 4:4). Also, Satan causes people to forget the Word of God by taking information out of their minds so that they will not be saved (Luke 8:12).

You may think you have never met a person who has had any contact whatever with demonic forces. But you've met yourself, and I suspect that is sufficient! No one can escape contact with the prince of the power of the air, the one who has organized his army of wicked spirits to fight God's people. Someone has said that Satan has already made meticulous plans for every believer's downfall. Think of it: A powerful evil spirit has already decided how he plans to ruin you!

Satan's Target

For centuries, philosophers and scientists have struggled with the problem of the nature of the mind. Questions such as: What are thoughts? What is the relationship between mind and matter? are puzzling. But this much seems clear: thoughts do not occupy space as we know it, but exist in a separate realm. For example, it would be absurd to speak of a thought as one inch long, or as occupying a specified area. Thoughts exist in a spiritual realm; your mind has entered into the spirit world.

Today we hear much about parapsychology and ESP. Undoubtedly the human mind does have natural powers that transcend ordinary experience. But herein lies a danger: because the mind operates in the spiritual realm, dabbling in matters such as ESP invites the influence and possible control of alien spirits. If you have been involved in any form of the occult and find yourself struggling with insidious forces, I suggest you read *The Adversary* by Mark Bubeck (Moody Press).

Satan does have access to the human mind; it exists in a realm that is not off-limits to spiritual forces, whether good or evil. Where did Judas get the idea to betray Christ? John said that the devil put the suggestion into the heart (mind) of Judas (John 13:2). Satan, you will recall, filled the minds of believers, namely Ananias and Sapphira, to lie to God. The mind—*your* mind—is the target of satanic attack. The adversary's method is to *drop ideas and suggestions into our minds so cleverly that we think these ideas are our own*. He inflames our passions, arouses greed, inflates our egos, and stirs up hatred and resentment. All of this and more is done by the roaring lion who stalks the earth, seeking whom he may devour. You can be sure that Satan is involved in the sin that is troubling you.

Does his activity absolve you from any responsibility in committing sin? Not in the least. Peter did not let Ananias and Sapphira off the hook because their lie was instigated by Satan.

Their untimely death stands as a reminder that they were responsible, even though Satan filled their hearts to lie to the Holy Spirit.

Or consider Judas. Satan entered him personally before the night of the betrayal. But the son of perdition paid dearly for that sin and will do so forever.

If you allow satanic activity in your life, God will hold you responsible, because you have the power to choose whether you will give territory to Satan's kingdom or not. Yes, Satan might suggest that you lie, but the choice whether to act on that suggestion is yours. He may suggest any sin imaginable, but ultimately you make the choice. He cannot work independently of your cooperation.

Dealing with the Devil

Some Christians reason, "If I leave Satan alone, he'll leave me alone. I don't want to get involved." Without realizing it, these believers have unwittingly conceded the battle to the enemy. Satan has them exactly where he wants them, safely tucked away on the shelf labeled "Too Frightened to Fight." I tell such people, "You don't want to get involved? My friend, you are involved—you've just made peace with the enemy by refusing to do battle with him."

Satan's most successful weapon is fear. He'll make you believe that if you take his existence seriously, he will create havoc in your home or ruin your peace of mind. Don't believe this. Satan is a liar and the father of lies (John 8:44). He will bluff you, pushing you as far as your ignorance will allow. But you have the authority to renounce Satan's foothold in your life. First, you must take inventory and check your armor. If there is one piece missing, you are vulnerable. One exposed area, and that's where an arrow will be coming through! Satan is an expert marksman. His arrows don't miss their target; you can't depend on a sloppy defensive attack to get you by unscathed. This is one war in which good luck doesn't count.

We can't discuss all seven pieces of armor here, but they are listed in Ephesians 6:12–17. Let me comment on only one: the breastplate of righteousness. Satan always needs some reason to trouble you, some sin that gives him a right to your life. Once that sin is confessed and forsaken, his foothold disintegrates. He still will attack, but you need not fall for his enticements.

There are people who are under satanic attack. They feel uncomfortable when someone even mentions the blood of Christ. But usually it is because they have wandered into Satan's territory by refusing to deal thoroughly with their past. Righteousness shields us from demonic attack. Satanic arrows are deflected when up against a conscience void of offense. If you are troubled by satanic attack, you should ask: Where have I given ground for Satan's attack? What sin has not been taken care of? Where do I resist God? Personal righteousness, then, is essential in sealing yourself off from Satan's activity. But so are the other pieces of armor listed in Ephesians. They are enumerated at the end of this chapter for your study.

Second, you need to realize that Satan has no rights, but won't admit it. Christ's death and ascension effectively cut the ground from under him. Before His death, Christ predicted, "Now judgment is upon this world; now the ruler of this world shall be cast out" (John 12:31). Christ's death and ascension to heaven won a legal victory over all satanic forces—Christ entered Satan's territory and won a decisive victory on the devil's home turf. Paul wrote regarding Christ, "When He had disarmed the rulers and authorities, He made a public display of them, having triumphed over them through Him" (Col. 2:15). That's why James can say, "Submit therefore to God. Resist the devil and he will flee from you" (4:7). Satan is allowed to maneuver through the atmosphere, causing havoc. But he can be successfully resisted. Paul wrote, "Be angry, and yet do not sin; do not let the sun go down on your anger, and do not give the devil an opportunity" (Eph. 4:26–27). You can say No to Satan!

Satan is like a dethroned king who keeps on giving orders to his subjects; he is like a thief who has stolen virtually everything he owns and who tries to persuade you that it was always his. He is like a warrior without authority who keeps recruiting mercenaries to fight a battle he has already lost!

Finally, remember that all believers have legal authority over demonic forces. There is a connection between Ephesians 1 and 2 that is often overlooked. Near the end of the first chapter, we read of God's great power which was displayed in Christ: "He raised Him from the dead and seated Him at His right hand in the heavenly places, far above all rule and dominion, and every name that is named, not only in this age, but also in the one to come. And He put all things in subjection under His feet, and gave Him as Head over all things to the church, which is His body, the fulness of Him who fills all in all" (Eph. 1:20–23).

I hope you read these verses carefully enough to see (1) that Christ's ascension to heaven placed Him above all rule, authority, power, and every name that is named; and (2) that all things are under His feet—no power exists in the universe without Christ's permission.

And here is the good news that puts it all together: in chapter 2, Paul says you are *seated with Christ* in heavenly places. This means that Satan, along with all of his wicked spirits, at this very moment is under your feet!

Sometimes Christians pray, "O Lord, we ask you to bind Satan; we pray that you would cause him to depart. . ." But resisting and binding Satan is *our* responsibility.

Often you feel weak and helpless, but this does not diminish your position of authority. A policeman may not feel strong at all; indeed, he may be ill or very tired. Physically, he would not be able to stop the smallest compact car. Yet when he raises his hand, all the traffic stops. Why? Because the state has given him authority over traffic.

I've heard people say, "I hear voices that tell me to commit suicide. I'm afraid that one of these days I'll do it." You need not listen to those voices. Satan cannot program you to obey his commands. The message of the New Testament is clear: Christ won a complete victory over Satan and we can now participate in that triumph.

Demonic Activity and Your Sinful Habit

How do we confront wicked powers? We follow the example of Christ, who commanded, "Be gone, Satan, in Jesus name, for it is written . . ." Use this statement, out loud if you are alone, and command Satan to depart, based on the promises of Scripture you have claimed. Remember that simply quoting a verse of Scripture does not make demonic forces cringe, but *the power of the Word of God is unleashed when you bring yourself under its authority*. The disciples could not cast out a demon because of unbelief and pride. They were ineffective because their lives were no longer under God's authority (Matt. 17:15–20).

Let's be specific. Suppose your habit is overeating. You've digested all the food your body really needs, but there is more in the refrigerator. You know that your body belongs to God, but the idea of eating keeps popping into your mind. You've memorized verses, given your struggle completely to God, and mapped out a simple diet program. But you just love to eat whether your body needs it or not. You close the refrigerator door, partially satisfied with your victory. But, you'll be back shortly.

Could your struggle have anything to do with demonic forces? Absolutely! The first sin occurred when Eve ate what she wasn't supposed to. Satan struck at the legitimate desire for food, and made the forbidden fruit enticing. In twentieth century language,

Eve could not close the door of her refrigerator. The food looked and smelled *so* good.

You're sitting on the sofa reading a magazine. The pictures of beautifully prepared foods make you think you're hungry. The idea to eat is powerful. Right now your mind is a battlefield. Satan has built a stronghold (2 Cor. 10:4–5). You will have to gain control over your thoughts. You must recognize them for what they are and say, "Satan, in the name of Jesus, I command you to leave me, for it is written, 'For God has not given us a spirit of timidity, but of power and love and discipline' " (2 Tim. 1:7). Insist upon that promise in Jesus' name. If you do, Satan will flee from you (James 4:7).

The same strategy must be used in resisting sexual temptation. Satan wants a foothold on your will. At first he is satisfied with only a tiny bit of control; time is on his side. If you give in a little he'll eventually get more. Sooner or later, you'll be a slave—that's all he wants.

When you resist him you will find relief, but probably not for long. Satan and his henchmen do not give up easily. Christ was confronted three times in rapid succession. If Satan assaults you 10 times, resist him 10 times, but don't give in. You have authority over every suggestion of the evil one.

I remember a battle that raged intermittently in my mind for nearly two hours. I resisted satanic forces, refocused my thoughts on God's promises only to be rebuffed again. So it went back and forth; the sinful thoughts left only to return. But because I kept insisting on my authority in Jesus' name and commanding the evil one to depart, those thoughts eventually left. Then, peace came to me.

Don't misunderstand. I've not seen the last of insidious thoughts. But whenever they return, they do so with less power, and I know that on the basis of Christ's authority I can insist on my freedom.

Don't ever be fooled when satanic forces withdraw. They never leave a believer alone because they have given up on him. If they withdraw, it is to regroup; it is to re-evaluate their next planned attack. Our responsibility is to be ready, guarding our heart and mind with all diligence, lest we become lax in the middle of a declared war.

Let me warn you that you may lose many battles, but eventually you will win the war. Slowly your victories will begin to outnumber your defeats. You'll discover that you do have authority, just as the Scriptures teach you. You will wrestle effectively against the kingdom of darkness and prove the Scripture which says, "Greater is He who is in you than he who is in the world" (1 John 4:4).

Suggested Application

1. If Satan wanted to destroy you—and he does—how would he do it? What sin in your life is the most likely place for him to attack?

2. Here are the seven pieces of armor listed in Ephesians 6:12–17. Included is a brief description of what each piece ought to mean to us personally.

    a. The belt of truthfulness: an attitude of complete honesty.

    b. The breastplate of righteousness: all sin must be confessed and we must constantly look to Christ who is our righteousness.

    c. The feet shod with the preparation of the Gospel of peace: an eagerness to present the Gospel whenever possible.

    d. The shield of faith: a life lived with implicit trust in God's Word.

    e. The helmet of salvation: confidence in the hope of salvation and the sufficiency of the Cross.

    f. The sword of the Spirit: knowing the specific statements of God to apply at the point of temptation.

    g. Pray always: a prayerful attitude of thankfulness and dependence.

        What steps do you plan to take to put on any missing pieces?

3. In addition to using Scripture as suggested in the chapter, we must learn to pray against demonic activity in our families, church, and also in specific individuals. We can do this best by putting on the armor of God daily and rebuking satanic activity by the use of Scripture.

A sample prayer might be:

Father, I thank You that Jesus Christ has ascended far above all principalities and powers. We rejoice that because we are joined to Him, we participate in His victory. I thank You that Satan and his armies have been defeated and must be subject to our exalted Saviour. Now in Jesus name, I ask that Satan's activity be stopped in the life of _____. I bring the mighty truth of my Lord's victory against all of Satan's workings in _____. I desire to be in fellowship with the Father, Son, and Holy Spirit throughout this day. I offer this prayer to God, in the name of the Lord Jesus Christ. Amen.

12

TRAPPED AGAIN

You have made some progress in tackling that sin that won't budge. Maybe you've gone for a day or even a week without slipping back into the same habit. You're pretty satisfied that finally you have seen light at the end of the tunnel. You are beginning to feel better about yourself and you're optimistic.

Then WHAM! Suddenly, you're back to Square 1. You've sinned. Here you thought you had it licked, and then it exploded in your face. You're tempted to conclude that you were deluded. Just like you suspected: victory isn't possible after all.

We've all tasted victory and later gagged on defeat. We've stood up—only to fall back on the same slippery slope. We've all wondered whether we should ever get up again.

What happened? Several things, possibly. Jerry G. Dunn, a former alcoholic, discovered a cycle among alcoholics (*God Is for the Alcoholic,* Chicago: Moody Press, 1975). As I've studied it, I've concluded that it is a cycle that all of us experience in one form or another. Dunn did a lot of thinking and praying to find out why alcoholics would quit drinking, go into a period of abstinence, and then return to drinking. God gave him insight into this problem, and that's when he noticed the cycle. Dunn says it can take a week, a month, or even years to complete the cycle.

First, the alcoholic desires never to take another drink. He's "had it." Never again will he make a fool of himself—waking up in a strange room, not knowing how he got there. Just remembering the *humiliation* of the past keeps him sober for a while.

Such a feeling is usually the first step toward freedom from any sin. You are tired of gaining weight, blowing your stack, or whatever. You become so weary of failure that you begin to seek a way of deliverance. So many Christians haven't come this far yet! They are still not fed up with their sin. Some of the more obnoxious habits may go, but not the subtle ones! Some sinful habits are still too attractive to discard completely. As we've already stressed, God wants you to desire victory for reasons other than personal fulfillment. But usually, your quest for freedom begins with a healthy disgust for your failures.

Second, Dunn noticed that alcoholics begin to take *pride* in their sobriety. They'll say, "You know, I haven't had a drink in three weeks." The alcoholic begins to feel better—he might even get his job back and regain the respect of his children. Soon he begins to have a superior attitude when watching his friends drink. He thinks to himself, "I'd never act that foolishly again, thank God." Yet it is difficult for him to avoid the constant bombardment of alcohol. Social drinking is accepted, and his friends invite him to join. He is still proud of his abstinence and yet fears that he just might slip back into his former habit. Dunn says, "This is the area we call 'a dry drunk.' This man has reached the place where he has to fight against taking another drink. He is disgusted with people who drink. He can't stand the smell of liquor. He becomes irritable and someone's suggestion that he take another drink becomes a personal insult."

But after enduring the struggle for some time, the alcoholic begins to think he has solved the problems which have caused his addiction. He feels better physically and mentally. Perhaps he has even begun to attend church, so he thinks his spiritual life is in order. He breathes a sigh of relief. At last, everything will be all right.

The next stage comes when he feels he has finally mastered the situation. At last, he has his problem under *control*. Opportunities to drink are just as numerous as ever. One of his associates says, "Aw, you can handle it." Until now, he has been refusing such offers. But now, he feels he is the master of a whole new world. Surely he is able to handle a single drink. So he says Yes—just once.

At this point, Dunn says, the alcoholic goes in one of two directions. If he is able to stop at one drink, he confirms his conclusion that he can handle drinking. He loses his fear of alcohol. He finds it easy to take another drink when it is offered.

Or that one drink might inflame his passion for alcohol. Dunn writes, "One drink might be enough to plunge him to the very depths of alcoholism as quickly as one can be pushed over a cliff."

Either way, the end result is the same: he will become completely victimized by the bottle again. Dunn mentions a doctor who completed the cycle in 10 years. By drinking a half-glass of beer, he started on another binge which eventually ruined his home and cost him his practice.

Your problem may not be alcoholism but my guess is that your cycle follows the same pattern. At least I've gone through the same steps with other sins. I've gone full circle. Let's take a look at what we can learn from our failures.

What Does God Want to Teach Us?

God uses our failures to teach us several lessons. The moment we fail, we receive a crash course in theology. We are vividly reminded that pride comes before a fall. Bunyan was right when he said, "He that is low need fear no fall."

Remember the Israelites at Ai? They had just conquered Jericho, a city fortified with huge, strong walls. God had just done a miracle; the walls had collapsed. The next city on their agenda was the smaller town of Ai. Fresh from the victory of Jericho, the men decided that only a small contingent would be needed to conquer the city. But Israel was defeated. Israel's self-confidence was ill-founded. In their enthusiasm for victory, they had overlooked the sin that was in the camp. Their past victory was no guarantee for future conquests.

We must learn that our most dangerous moment is when we think we have finally mastered our situation. A series of victories sets us up for a fall. Not one of us should ever say, "This is one sin I have under control. I'll never commit it again."

God loathes self-righteousness, a superior, judgmental attitude. How easy it is to say, "I'd never do what he did!" Anyone who says that has no idea of what he is capable of doing. There is no sin beyond the capacity of any one of us. If we've not succumbed to the same degree of evil as others, it is because we have not had the same opportunities to do evil, and more importantly, because God's grace has restrained us.

Remember the Pharisee who went into the temple to pray? He's generally remembered for reciting all of his good works to God. But what we often overlook is that he didn't take the credit for his performance—at least he said, "God, I thank *Thee* that I am not like other people . . ." (Luke 18:11). But although he *thanked God* he was not like others, he did not receive God's mercy. Why? Because even *good works done in God's name are never the basis for God's acceptance of us*. The publican, the tax-gatherer, was accepted precisely because he understood that *the basis of His acceptance was God's mercy alone*.

Even the oft-repeated assertion (usually recited by well-dressed Christians who occasionally visit Skid Row), "There but for the grace of God go I," can be said self-righteously. We think we are different, better than others, because we have attracted God's favor. Even such refined self-righteousness is anathema to God. He wants us to see that *in essence,* all human beings are the same. If we are objects of His special grace, it is because of His sovereign pleasure; it's not because we are better.

Our failures help us learn these lessons. I don't know what Paul's thorn in the flesh was, but it originated with the devil. He says it was "a messenger of Satan to buffet me—to keep me from exalting myself!" (2 Cor. 12:7b) Yet that weakness was expressly allowed by God to keep Paul from self-righteousness.

God does not cause us to sin, but He uses our sins to remind us of our weakness. We are less tempted to judge others, and more understanding, when we become well acquainted with the wickedness of our own heart. We then learn how to view others with humility, considering ourselves, lest we also be tempted. When we are caught by sin, God uses the experience to teach us about His righteousness and His hatred of sin.

God also wants us to appreciate the wonder of His grace; "Where sin increased, grace abounded all the more" (Rom. 5:20). Because of pride, I find it hard to admit that I need God's grace so continually, so desperately. How we'd all like to be able to say, "I've not committed that sin in 10 years." But our continual problems with sin crowd us to the Cross. Again and again, we are confronted with Calvary; we are forced to come with nothing in our hands to receive God's provision freely given from His grace.

Peter summarizes it all for us by saying, "Clothe yourselves with humility toward one another, for God is opposed to the proud, but gives grace to the humble. Humble yourselves, therefore, under the mighty hand of God, that He may exalt you at the proper time" (1 Peter 5:5b–6).

Signposts to Failure

At Niagara Falls, there is a point of no return; a place where the water rushes so fiercely that it would be impossible to make progress against the stream. Going over the falls is inevitable. There are warning signs that tell the unwary where that point is, but some foolhardy souls either have ignored the signs or have not seen them. They're not around to tell us which it was.

We have our warning signs too. Generally, it's a slow leak and not a blowout that stops us. Failure, actually, is quite predictable. We can tell whether we are on our way to the point of no return.

What are those signposts? The first is *a feeling of self-satisfaction, a sigh of relief that finally we have everything under control.* At that moment, we are vulnerable because our confidence rests with ourselves and our past record rather than with the Lord. Remember the alcoholic? He thinks he has drinking under control. He must be reminded that he never has drinking under control. Even at Alcoholics Anonymous meetings, the participants are trained to say, "I *am* an alcoholic." And they must remember that even after they have been dry for 10 years!

Friend, you *are* a sinner. And you will be one until the day you die. Beware of thinking that you have any sin permanently under control. "Therefore let him who thinks he stands take heed lest he fall" (1 Cor. 10:12).

Then there is the danger of making hidden provision for defeat. Jerry wanted desperately to overcome his addiction to pornography, but he kept one obscene picture in his room, just in case he was tempted! Or consider the person who wants to stop smoking but keeps a pack of cigarettes in the drawer, thinking that he might need them! Your mind is like a huge house with many rooms. You might be willing to clean up the kitchen, living room, and even some of the bedrooms. But what about that closet crammed with junk? Perhaps it is precious to you, for it represents one small part of your life you are not willing to surrender to the searchlight of the Holy Spirit. But Christ wants to be the Master of your entire life. Everything that is hidden He wants to reveal. There is only one way you can meet Christ's requirement, and that is by refusing to have any room in your life that can be used to retreat to from your spiritual commitment.

God wants you to perform radical surgery on sinful habits. You must burn all bridges behind you. This is what Christ taught in the Sermon on the Mount. Immediately following His remark about the sin of lust, He made a shocking statement: "And if your right eye makes you stumble, tear it out, and throw it from you; for it is better for you that one of the parts of your body perish, than for your whole body to be thrown into hell. And if your right hand makes you stumble, cut it off and throw it from you; for it is better for you that one of the parts of your body perish, than for your whole body to go into hell" (Matt. 5:29–30).

Once an eye is cut out or a hand cut off, there is no chance of it being put back. The separation is final; there is no hidden agenda for a comeback. Paul wrote, "But put on the Lord Jesus Christ, and make no provision for the flesh in regard to its lusts" (Rom. 13:14).

Also, there is the signpost of spiritual coasting. That's what happens when we begin to crowd God and His Word to the circumference of our lives. This happens so subtly, unintentionally, as we feel more pressured by the responsibilities of life: job, spouse, children, hobbies, church, friends—and even television.

I've been on a boat that has left the shore so quietly that I scarcely noticed it. That's the way most backsliding happens, slowly and without fanfare. Only tragic failure makes us realize how far we have drifted from the shore. God prefers that we be either cold or hot, rather than lukewarm. The reason is simple: someone who is cold seeks the fire, a person who is lukewarm is generally comfortable and sees no need of change. He is so self-satisfied that he doesn't know how bad off he is! The people at Laodicea were lukewarm, but thought they were hot! They had drifted from their first love and *didn't even know it*. Beware of spiritual coasting!

Finally there is the signpost of compromise. That's when we tolerate personal sin for just a little while. I have seen a man shatter a cement wall with a huge hammer. The first time he hit it, the wall was as solid as ever. Even after 20 blows, it seemed immovable. But he kept at it. After a while, the wall weakened, but it still stood firm and upright. But it *was* weakening! A small piece fell, then another, and gradually it collapsed.

That's the way sin is. It is true that you can tolerate sin without having it ruin you—but you can't do that forever. Compromise is possible for a while without disastrous results, but eventually it weakens your resistance.

While writing this book, I have heard of a Christian leader who has been involved in the sin of adultery. Probably it began innocently enough—friendship, then a few fantasies and some lustful thoughts. But such escapades in the imagination *do* weaken a person's resistance. Like the cement wall, he can remain solid for a while, believing all is well. But eventually he collapses. Watch for these signposts. They are danger signals, warning of unseen rocks along the shore. Get back on course, keeping your eye on Jesus, the Author and Finisher of our faith (Heb. 12:2).

How Long Before You Stand Again?

You've been caught in the old trap, you're back in the same rut. How long should you stay there? Satan would like to say, "Forever. After all, what's the use—since you are not really sure you'll be victorious next time, why bother getting back into fellowship?"

You could be tempted to agree. Human nature resents the idea that we must come back to God without an "award for special merit" sign pinned on our vest. We are uncomfortable accepting mercy that we don't deserve. We hesitate to come back immediately without a period of probation. We may even want to punish ourselves for our guilt by maintaining isolation from God and His people. So we postpone our appointment with the Almighty until we have proved we mean business and that we will never fall again. Furthermore, we argue, guilt is good for us; it will teach us *never* to do that again!

God thinks otherwise. For one thing, even if we do reform, that is not His basis for our acceptance anyway. To think we must straighten up before we come back to Him betrays our misunderstanding of the Cross. We are to come solely on the merit of the blood, not on the merit of an acceptable track record.

And is guilt good for us? True, it teaches us how uncomfortable the after effects of sin can be, but it's doubtful whether guilt is an acceptable motivation to change our behavior. At any rate, nowhere in the Bible do we read that God uses guilt to discipline His children. Natural consequences of sin, Yes, for they teach us how reprehensible sin can be. But guilt is not God's means of discipline, because it is contrary to the Cross. God's method of motivating us to live righteously is His love and grace. Listen to Paul: "I urge you therefore, brethren, by the *mercies of God,* to present your bodies a living and holy sacrifice, acceptable to God, which is your spiritual service of worship" (Rom. 12:1, italics added). Grace, freely given, does not provide us license to sin; rather, it should motivate us to give ourselves without reservation to the One who loves us so freely, so deeply. Whenever you sin, God wants you to come back into fellowship *immediately*. Learn your lessons, but within His forgiveness, not outside of it.

Sometimes we hear that we should "keep short accounts with

God.'' It's a way of reminding us not to let sin pile up in our lives. Don't think that you have to wait until the church doors open, or even until the end of the day, before sin is cared for. Confess it *the moment it is brought to your attention*. In fact, don't keep short accounts with God, but keep *current* accounts with God. While you are driving your car, working in the office, or doing chores at home, you can be engaging in dialogue with God. As you speak to Him, He replies through His Word.

Listen to the hope of the Scriptures for all who sin:

Thus says the Lord, "Do men fall and not get up again? Does one turn away and not repent?" (Jer. 8:4)

The Lord sustains all who fall, and raises up all who are bowed down (Ps. 145:14).

Do not rejoice over me, O my enemy. Though I fall, I will rise; though I dwell in darkness, the Lord is a light for me (Micah 7:8).

For a righteous man falls seven times, and rises again (Prov. 24:16).

The steps of a man are established by the Lord; And He delights in his way. When he falls, he shall not be hurled headlong; Because the Lord is the One who holds his hand (Ps. 37:23–24).

You can say No to that stubborn habit by saying Yes to God once again!

Suggested Application

1. Think back to the last time you were trapped by your weakness. Did you have any indication that you were going to give in to the temptation? What can you learn from this experience?

2. In what ways do we sometimes entertain temptation, thinking that we can handle it and know where to stop? What does this type of attitude show about our lives?

3. What do you think might be the best antidote to drifting in our spiritual lives? Or are there *several* precautions that are needed? Think of ways that we can lessen the chances of spiritual stumbling?

4. Why do we often delay our confession of sin after we have sinned? What lessons have we not yet learned?

5. Ponder this question: Why is sin so subtle?

13

WRITING THE LAST CHAPTER

You have now read and pondered the basic principles which God can use to renew your mind and change your behavior. Where do you go from here? What can you do to follow through on any commitment you have made?

This book is incomplete unless it is applied; we must not only *know* the truth but *do* it. For this reason, *you* will write the last chapter! Most of us do not need more truth than we already have; what we need is to weave what we know into the fabric of our own daily lives. So here is your opportunity to take over where this book leaves off. You will decide how this book will end in the way you deal with temptation.

To write the last chapter, purchase a thick notebook. It will belong to you alone—no editor will read its contents to see if it is marketable. No need to review your grammar or use a dictionary or check your spelling. This chapter is between you and God.

This notebook will become your *Spiritual Diary,* a chronicle of where you are in the Christian life, where you want to be, and the steps you'll take to get there. Of course, you will write whatever you wish in your book, but I am including some suggestions that you may want to incorporate into your *Diary.*

1. Write a letter to God, telling Him

    a. about your past—the failures and the successes. Be sure to include your weaknesses, or bad habits.

    b. Share with God the desires of your heart. Specifically, tell Him what you would like to have Him do in your life during the next five years, the next year, the next month. Concentrate on character qualities, remembering that His goal is that you be conformed to the image of His Son.

2. Write out special prayer requests for others: your partner, children, relatives, friends. Be specific.

3. Ask God to give you wisdom to outline a strategy to become the person you believe He wants you to be. This will include items such as beginning each day with God, memorizing two or more verses of Scripture a week; learning the ministry of intercession for others.

4. Try to anticipate the ways that Satan and the flesh will attempt to prevent you from following through with your commitment, such as sleeping too late, watching TV, being disorganized. Minimize the possibility that you will fail. How much is a disciplined relationship with God worth to you?

5. Regularly record in your notebook items such as:

    a. specific prayer requests *and* their answers.

    b. special observations you make on the Scriptures which are of particular help.

    c. the lessons which God teaches you.

Let your book become a monument to God's faithfulness in your life. If you do, the most important chapter in this book will be the last one, the one which *you* are writing. The Apostle Paul acknowledged that the best book is a life lived in the power of the Spirit, "You are our letter, written in our hearts, known and read by all men" (2 Cor. 3:2).

May God help you to begin *today*.